HUNA

Ancient Miracle Healing Practices
and the
FUTURE OF MEDICINE

By

Allen Lawrence, M.D., Ph.D.
Lisa Lawrence, M.S.

Hanover House
New York

A HANOVER TRADE PAPERBACK
Published by
Hanover House
a division of the
Zinn Publishing Group:
ZINN COMMUNICATIONS / NEW YORK

ISBN: 0-935016-14-7

Printed in the United States of America

Library of Congress Cataloging-in-Publication Data

Lawrence, Allen L.
  ''Huna'' ancient miracle healing practices and the
Future of medicine / by Allen Lawrence, Lisa Lawrence.
     p.   cm
  Includes bibliographical references.
  ISBN 0-935016-14-7
  1. Huna. I. Lawrence, Lisa. II. Title.
RZ999.L35   1994
615.8'52—dc20   94-38719
                                               CIP

HUNA

Hanover House
ZINN COMMUNICATIONS
New York

HUNA

Table of Contents

Acknowledgements

We would like to thank Mary Embree, our editor and friend, for all her assistance and input. This book could not have been done without her invaluable help.

We would also like to acknoeledge and thank Sally Leizerowitz and Todd Lawrence for their advice and support. Jim and Rosalie Heacock for believing in this book and the good job that they have done for us.

Finally, we are grateful to our families for putting up with us, loving us and cheering us on during the process of writing this book.

Foreword

■ This book for the first time presents a full account of how the medical profession can integrate the Huna system into its regular medical practice with better results than with standard medical modalities alone. Dr. Lawrence is a medical doctor who uses Huna in his own practice and explains how to do it.

Max Freedom Long envisioned Huna as an effective, complementary system that would help people to live healthy, happy, and productive lives. He saw in Huna psychological techniques a useful tool that would help individuals be more effective in every area of their lives, which in turn would be a boon to society. From the very beginning of the recovery of the ancient wisdom more than seventy years ago, a few medical doctors have recognized the importance of the Huna philosophy as a useful adjunct to their specialized medical practice. Long referred to these as "medical doctors who are also healers." Some of their experiences in using Huna methods along with standard medical techniques are reported in his research bulletins.

Dr. Lawrence suggests a solution to the problem of health care: "Don't Get Sick!" He sees Huna as "a way of thinking that can decrease your chances of illness and improve the health of your entire family." This book is about helping you get well and stay healthy, thus preventing the need of intervention from medical practitioners. "Huna creates a system which can virtually be entirely free of guilt, shame, confusion and fear – all of the conditions that commonly lead to illness and disease." The emphasis is on using the Huna philosophy and techniques within the present medical system. That is a most important focus and one which has been advocated by Huna practitioners from the beginning.

More and more doctors are becoming realistically open to changing the way they practice medicine to include true prevention and including their patients as partners in the process of creating wellness. Well people don't believe in illness. Unfortunately, "too many doctors do believe in illness" and, when this mindset is accepted by doctor and patient, the result is keeping people sick.

Using Huna does not require stopping standard medical care, whether prescribed medication or necessary surgery. Rather by using Huna along with your current care program, you can add to and facilitate your healing and wellness. Huna healing involves every level of body, mind, and spirit. It includes any medical treatment that is appropriate to a rational, middle-self decision of professionals in consultation with the patient. It includes the power of emotions and right attitudes from the lower self or subconscious. It also includes the element of "prayer-actions" involving the Higher Self or spiritual dimension of both patient and doctor in bringing about healing.

The physician who uses his medical skill along with mentally directed energy, knowing the make-up of not only the physical body, but the Huna concept of the body, can significantly increase his "power" to heal. No longer does he need only to treat; he can now use the power he gains through this ancient wisdom to empower his ability to heal his patients of the problems which cause their illnesses.

The process of modern medicine is to diagnosis illness and treat it. This implies that the person must get sick, so that the doctor can intervene. Huna does not require the individual to get sick for it to work.

As Dr. Lawrence says, "Huna is ultimately about wellness."

— E. Otha Wingo, Ph.D.
Executive Director,
Huna Research, Inc.,
1760 Anna Street,
Cape Girardeau, MO 63701-4505
(314) 334-3478

Introduction

■ "I'm so tired of being sick, won't someone please help me?" I cannot tell how many times I have heard cries for help such as these throughout my years in medical practice. Each of us as physicians find ourselves from time to time with a patient who doesn't seem to be getting help from the medical system.

Sometimes we ourselves feel helpless because we want to help so much. Other times it is clear that the patient himself has not been following instructions and in fact may even be recalcitrant and unwilling to do what is necessary to get well. Generally, few physicians stop and think that possibly our medical approach to these patients may be wrong. These patients may require anapproach that the physician himself may not yet even be aware of or has not had the opportunity to try. It is possible that standard medicine cannot help every patient; that on occasion, we must go beyond medicine as it is generally practiced. The physician may ask himself, "How could it be possible that with all our training and all our experience we are not able to solve so many of the medical and health problems we see in daily practice? How is it that we are so frequently unable to cure our patients? How is it that the majority of the time we are only capable of treating our patient's symptoms, and not the real problem behind them, so that, at least temporarily, we can reduce their pain or discomfort?" The patient on the other hand may be asking, "How could it be that so many physicians have no sense of what we, as patients, really need to prevent us from getting sick or at least to help us get better from the illnesses we find ourselves subjected to? How is it that so many physicians do not even recognize that the treatments they use don't really work?"

While physician and patient ask these questions, we as advocates of wellness and healing should ask another question. "Why is it that our physicians are generally willing to treat problems after the patient has become sick instead of preventing illness in the first place?" While the answers to these questions remain generally undealt with by our society, it appears thatthese problems and methodologies of healing have been dealt with by another, ancient society. Huna, the secret healing knowledge of the Polynesians, is a religio-spiritual healing system that is older than our modern medical system and has answers to many of our questions built directly into it.

The exact origins of Huna lie somewhere in the dawn of man. It is not a science in the sense that there is a body of literature, articles and journals where we can find how each tenet was decided upon. Yet it grants us an understanding of the human psyche and body that works to both prevent and create physical and emotional illness. While there has not been a large body of published material about it, what does exist demonstrates its simplicity and workability. Some might say that you would have to accept it on faith alone; however, this is the same even with modern medicine.[1] I believe that just about any astute, open-minded individual could quickly see that Huna makes sense and works. Some skeptics might say that it is a religion and hence works only on belief and faith. This might be true but not in the sense we commonly think of. In Huna there is no specific deity to pray to;there is no specific dogma to believe in. As sin is one of the most important principles in Huna, it is the only one aspect that would fit into the concept of religion. Contrary, however, to most other religions, Huna believes that there is one and only one sin, the intentional injury or hurt of another or of the self. This and its concept of integration of the mind, body and spirit – and a lot of common sense – are the basis of Huna.

Another point which may raise the eyebrows of doubters is that there are a number of rituals involved in Huna. These rituals which will be discussed in a later section are not religious rituals in the ordinary way we think of them. They are more like the process one might elect to go through to impress the inner self that he really means business and has the right intentions. Disbelievers might also think that Huna contains magic. If magic is defined as an occurrence without reproducible proof or out of thin air or as an illusion, this is not true. If magic is defined as the hidden power of the mind-body to create miracles then Huna indeed is about magic. Huna has been shown to heal problems modern medicine has been unable to heal.

While the goal of the physician should be to get his patient well, much too often he settles for merely treating his patient. The use of Huna allows the physician to work with his patient to create a cure.

Huna, once thought of as magic, is in actuality an extremely sophisticated healing system. It works with the nature of man rather than subjecting him to drugs, chemicals and surgical treatment. Healing through Huna is based on what is now being found to be many of the principles of *psychoneuroimmunobiology*. This field of medicine recognizes that there is not only a strong interrelationship between mind and body but that mind, body and the Universe itself are really one and the same. The realization of the fact that the immune system is directly under the control of the mind will change the way that medicine will be practiced in the future. While psychoneuroimmunobiology is a relatively new branch of modern medical science, the concepts are extremely old. They in fact, not only predate modern medicine, but have existed since the earliest days of life in this Universe. Huna and medicine are, in a sense, one and the same thing. Fritjov Capra, in his book the *Tao of Physics*, suggested that the ancient scriptures, the Vedas and the Upanashads, stated in words what modern physists were now finding in the laboratory. The ancients, not having a sophisticated mathematics, wrote down the laws of Quantum physics in their "religious books." Hence, the ancient used words to describe what the more contemporary scientists are proving mathematically. In a sense the same is true of the relationship of Huna and medicine.

While the exact source of Huna is still unclear, there is little question in my mind that Huna has its origins in the "spiritual mysteries." For those who have not previously been introduced to the "mysteries" this would take a book on its own. However, simply stated, these mysteries are the secrets of life which were taught to worthy students who in turn teach others. The purpose was to tell those who would rule and govern, write, and heal what the true nature of the Universe is about.

While the specific origin and teachings of the mysteries are shrouded in the antiquities of time, it is clear these were not just primitive rites where priests learned religion. They were where ancient scientists and seekers learned and passed on their knowledge of the Universe. It may well be that the secret of these mysteries lies in the legendary source of mankind, the "Motherland of Man." This was the lost continent of Mu which flourished for over one hundred thousand years and was destroyed in the "Great Magnetic Cataclysms" that took place some twenty thousand years ago. Others say that the mysteries began with the building of the Temple of Solomon.

No matter what its origin, Huna embodies a wisdom that leaves a trail through Egypt, the Mosaic (Old Testament) Bible, the New Testament, the teachings of Jesus, Gnostic Christian traditions, Hippocratic laws, the Code of Hamarabe, modern psychoneuroimmunobiology, quantum physics, modern psychology and, as stated earlier, modern medicine. Whether Huna is the survivor or the great-grandchild is unknown. However, its application to healing and modern medicine is significant and never more relevant than today. It is clear that Huna was developed long before modern surgical and drug treatments existed. The ancient Masters of Huna, the Kahunas, needed to heal injuries, illnesses and disease just as we do today. Without the ability to heal the injured and ill there would be loss of life there which could threaten the very survival of the group.

Huna was developed as a natural extension of the day-to-day work of healers, shamans and physicians in solving problems and healing their patients. With time the ancients discovered that their role as healer could be passed down from parent to child. It is likely that Huna is a science thousands of years old.

These ancient Huna priests and healers no longer exist. They have been replaced by the technological physician. However, the knowledge of the essence of man and how he heals and creates wellness still exists and flourishes in the "science" of Huna. As medicine moves more andmore to technological excellence, we more than ever before need the humanistic touch of Huna.

SECTION I

MEDICINE AND THE MODERN ART OF TREATING

CHAPTER ONE

The State of Medical Practice Today

The state of the practice of medicine in the United States has never been better and never been worse. In recent years politicians and the general public have made known their dissatisfaction with the escalating cost of medical services and the declining quality of health care. Few people, physicians or general public, are entirely happy with it. Yet, in the technical aspects of medical care, researchers continue to make astounding breakthroughs into the areas of diagnostics, surgical treatments and medical technologies.

With all its advances however, medicine has made little or no progress on the human level. The main problem that plagues the medical profession is the growing gap between physician and patient. It is not at all uncommon to hear people ask, "Do physicians really care?" One person recently told me, "Whenever I go to my doctor I wait for hours to see him and then he only spends a few minutes with me." This person was unhappy not just because her doctor didn't have a great deal of time to give her but also because, "he never answers any of my questions." Twenty years ago a physician spent the greatest portion of his day with his patients. He had time to listen and often became a friend to his patient. Not unlike the Huna master, he made house calls and entered into the world of his patient. He had the opportunity to see how his patient lived and the circumstances of his life, his family, his neighborhood and often even his friends. Frequently, he even became part of the family.

Today a major portion of the physician's time is spent in preparing the mountains of paperwork, medical charts, reports, insurance forms, legal forms and correspondences that are now required to get payment and manage the patient's case. Generally, this either requires a substantial portion of his day, or he must hire someone who can do this work for him. In either case, he must work harder. If he does it himself, he must either do it after seeing his patients or over the weekends. This leaves him less free time for himself or his family. If he tries to do it within the work day he must see less patients. If he hires someone (or gets an expensive computer system to do it for him), which isgenerally what happens, he must work more hours or see more patients in each work hour to be able to pay these salaries and costs of doing business. Ultimately, this bureaucracy of medicine is not only costly to the physician and his personal time, but takes him away from his patients. It also substantially increases the cost of the practice of medicine. This cost is then necessarily passed on to the patient in the form of higher medical bills as well as less personal contact, a more distant relationship and less involvement. In the end both the physician and his patient suffer. Rather than working together in a partnership to provide and protect health, they often become adversaries.

In virtually every medical school some students are studying medicine because they want to help people. Others clearly are studying medicine simply for the money they believe they can make as a physician. The majority of physicians, even those looking to make money at being a physician, hold the welfare of their patient in high esteem. Few people are willing to go through the rigors of a medical education only to make money. It seems quite illogical to spend 12 to 14 years in college, medical school, internship and a residency training program and to pay the fees it costs to do this only to end up doing it for the money. Yet in recent years more and more physicians have confessed to us that money is now the only thing they have left. Their capacity to take care of their patients is now almost completely dominated byhospitals, committees, insurance companies and the government.

Many young physicians who have just entered the practice of medicine accept the present day circumstances of medicine in their stride. After all, most have no idea of the way it was. The older physicians, however, often find this increasingly difficult. Many physicians who initially went into the field of medicine for the purpose of healing and helping the sick feel lost and empty. They often have let go their desire for getting their patients well and have become involved in charity work or hobbies. They are literally forced to turn away from what they can't have to what they can have. Many physicians are now depressed, stressed and frustrated without knowing why. The changes that have enveloped medicine, while only taking a few years, have occurred so insidiously that they were not seen by many physicians until it was too late. Worse, the changes that occurred were entirely out of their hands. There was little they could say or do about it. Changes often took long periods of time to be set in motion. By the time they were in place the physicians were frequently already used to them. Deluged with so many changes, new regulations, new ways of doing things, the effects of legislation, hospital and insurance company requirements the physician has had little time to think about what was coming and what had transpired.

At this point the American public has virtually lost touch with their family physician. More and more individuals are seeking attention in urgent care facilities and emergency rooms. Their insurance companies are now telling them who they can and who they can't see. The closeness of patient and his doctor and their ability to communicate with each other has ultimately been lost. Just as the physician has lost his autonomy, the general public has lost its freedom to choose and to get what they want. With the increasing costs of medical care there have also been a substantial increase in the number of mega-corporations getting into the arena of providing health care services. Now, rather than a friendly neighborhood doctor, people are learning to get used to the mega-medical clinic.

More and more medicine is now being practiced with a corporate heart. The bottom line is now much more important than the individual's needs. Costs are being cut by reducing physicians and nurses salaries, using entry level employees in areas which call for skilled personnel, and by using generic medications instead of the more costly and reliable name brands. Surgical procedures, both major and minor, are being controlled not simply by need but by budgetary considerations. In order for an indicated surgery to be performed it must be approved in advance. Approval can sometimes take weeks or even months. Seeing the same doctor is almost extinct. People often see a different doctor at every visit. Commonly the doctor knows nothing about the patient. Frequently, he hasn't the time to read through the notes of the last doctor to find out what the patient is coming back for. If all this is not enough, we are paying more for our medical care than we ever have before and it is harder than ever to get insurance.

"It can't possibly get worse?" you say. Well, that all depends. We are presently sitting on the verge of substantial changes in the health care system. In the near future, legislative force will be put behind reducing the cost of medical care and hopefully opening medical care to hundreds of thousands, maybe millions of people who now cannot afford it. It is possible that these changes will impact positively on the health care system but it is more likely that it won't. As more new people with chronic illnesses enter into the system, the system already over-taxed, will not be able to handle them. Physicians may have less time than ever. If no system for preventing illness is put into place, it will not be long before medical care will become totally impersonal and much more of a formula.

What then are the options for you and your family? The best, and possibly, the only way out, *will be to not get sick at all*. We realize that this is a unique way of thinking but it is one that could literally solve everyone's problems. Not getting sick means you don't have to worry about seeingdoctors. If enough people were not getting sick the cost of medical care would drop. The physician would have fewer patients to work on. He would have more time to spend with those who did get sick. Your insurance cost could possibly be reduced and your income therefore increased. Best of all, not having to get sick is a realistic and relatively attainable possibility. In the past. when medical practices profited by illness, few doctors would have been willing to admit that it was possible. However, as the landscape is changing, more and more doctors are becoming realistically open to changing the way they practice medicine to include true prevention and to accept their patient as a partner in the process of creating wellness. In the following chapters we will introduce you to a way of thinking that can decrease your chances of illness and improve the health of your entire family.

This book is not about what is right or wrong with the medical profession. It is about helping you get well, helping you heal yourself when you're sick and preventing illness when you are healthy. If Huna was the predominant medical paradigm the job of the medical profession would be much easier. You would already know what we are about to tell you. This book is about using Huna philosophies and techniques within the present medical system. Todo this effectively there are some more things you must know and understand about the medical system.

THE PATIENT AND ILLNESS

To best understand why you may not be getting what you want or need from the medical profession, we must look briefly at their overall goals, how it is set up and what they are actually giving us. First, however, it is important to understand what the general public wants and asks from the medical profession.

When I originally entered into the practice of medicine I wanted to save lives, to help people and get people well. Over the years, however, I recognized that this was not happening very often. At first I blamed myself, I must not be doing my job well. Later, I realized that it was not entirely my problem. I found that I was seeing three different types of people as patients.

The first group was either frequently or always sick. They suffered from a number of acute and chronic diseases. These illnesses were most commonly based around occupations (back problems, injuries, carpal tunnel syndrome), addictions (alcoholism, use of tobacco, drugs), diabetes, heart disease, cancer, mental illness, emotional illness, autoimmune illnesses, infectious diseases (AIDS, tuberculosis) or injuries (automobile, home accidents, fires, etc.). Most of the disorders in this group were, in one way or another, related to *Stress*.

The second group were people who were sick only occasionally or even continuously sick but not severely. Their illnesses were considerably more evasive and tended to be primarily stress related illnesses, life-style problems, nutritional problems, spiritual conflicts and spiritual emergencies. In this group we saw conditions such as ulcers, anxiety, panic, high blood pressure, asthma and allergies. These illnesses were worsened with the circumstances of the individual's life. They often set up the context of the first group. When conditions worsen, the ability to resist declines, or the will to live and resist illness diminishes. Without proper treatment of their *real problems* it is not unusual for these people to progress into the ranks of those affected by the chronic diseases listed above.

The third group is populated by a rather large number of people who never or only rarely appear to get sick. It was this group that fascinated me over the many years I was in practice. It was because of these people that I learned what health and wellness are really about. It was also due to them that I finally recognized the underlying intent of the medical profession. What I have learned from this group is that illness is generally a state of mind. Again and again I would see certain patients for such things as a routine annual physical examination, for school physicals or job physicals, immunization, marriage certificate, etc. Not infrequently they would start their session by stating, "I don't like coming to doctors, but I had to this time. I don't believe in illness so fortunately I don't have to see doctors very often." Usually, after I would take care of whatever business was necessary, I would talk to them about their *lack of belief in illness*. Many of these people would tell me that they just never thought about getting ill.

They were too busy living their life and taking care of their business. Others would tell me that they had once been sick and that they had simply decided that they would never let that happen to them again. Here was a group which *actively* worked at not getting sick. They watched their diet, took vitamins and often meditated. Interestingly enough, many had been Christians who had left Christianity to join other religious affiliations, often with a more Eastern philosophical approach.

Beyond these attributes these people "who never got sick" often had little in common, some were rich, others poor, some on state aid, others insured by their jobs. There were men and women and occasionally even children. One thing, however, that they all seemed to have in common was they not only *didn't believe in illness* but they *totally believed in wellness and being well*. As one person put it, "I don't believe that illness exists. I believe that we can give power to the idea that it exists and once we do this we open ourself up for it to happen. Not because it is there but because our mind will make anything happen that we believe will happen. I have chosen to believe absolutely that I am well and will always be well. It works for me, that's all I can say."

One question which I asked over and over again netted a very interesting answer. *"WHY DON'T YOU LIKE GOING TO SEE DOCTORS?"* After all, most of the individuals in this group generally started their conversation with me by telling me that they didn't like going to doctors. The answer I most frequently was given was, **"I don't like going to doctors because most of them believe in illness."**

THE HIGH COST OF BELIEVING IN ILLNESS

Over a period of years I watched this in my own life. I observed myself as well as other medical doctors. What I found was that it is true. For the most part medical doctors not only *believe in illness, but they expect it and are disappointed when they don't find it. In fact, they frequently create it.* For example, when a patient comes to them with slightly elevated blood, pressure rather than looking for the factors in that person's life they tell him that his blood pressure is elevated and he is in danger. They then prescribe medications to it. Since they did not solve the problem that caused the elevated blood pressure, it is not unusual to see the process worsen over time. Another thing that happens commonly is that they take responsibility over the patient and his or her body. "I'm the doctor you must do as I say." In these situations, they take the power for healing away from the source. The individual turns his life and his body over to the doctor **who fully believes in the illness process.** Often doctors who don't find illness in their patient often lose interest in that patient. Frequently routine preventive health exams are treated as an imposition. Many patients have told me, and I have personally seen it myself, that when some doctors are asked to perform a preventive medical examination they perform very brief and perfunctory examinations. They are just not interested in prevention.

Finally, I have been told many times by patients and also seen for myself that many doctors refuse to educate their patients. Often they also refuse to answer legitimate questions. On one occasion while observing an examination as a resident, a staff physician was asked an intelligent question by the patient. He entirely ignored the question and when it was repeated stated firmly, "Madam, I ask the questions here." The major problem we face is that *the medical profession is actually designed to keep people sick.* I realize that this view does not make me popular with my medical colleagues but it is true. While there certainly are wonderful physicians who do care for and heal their patients most doctors just treat their patients and often never get anyone really well.

I am not suggesting that all or even most doctors are bad doctors. Quite the contrary, most doctors are very good doctors. They do the medical profession quite proud as the system is designed. They simply never get people well. They treat them with medications covering up theirpatient's problems and they convince their patients that they know what is in their best interest. The doctor tells his patient that if he follows his advice then his symptoms will be minimized and/or eliminated. Generally, the doctor gives what he promises. The patient survives his illness and not infrequently his symptoms are controlled or at least made better. However, the patient lives the rest of his life with his illness, taking medications and being under his doctor's care. The problem that caused his illness, however, may never actually be solved.

While the patient diligently takes his medications to control his symptoms and to feel better, he may often develop side effects from the medication. The physician then changes medications hoping to find one that works but produces less side effects. Often new medications become necessary to control the side effects and their symptoms. As time passes the patient may find that he is taking more and more medication until he is taking anywhere from two to ten different medications. Some to control the original problem. Some to control new problems that have arisen because the original problem was never solved and some to control the side effects from the other medications. While there are many sophisticated doctors who are able to understand the interaction of the medications they prescribe and the surgeries they perform, there are unfortunately many moredoctors who are not so sophisticated. These doctors aren't always aware of the full implications of the drugs they use, the side effects they create and the long term affect on their patients. They are often not even aware of the problems their patients face until some catastrophic crisis occurs.

Possibly more damning than anything said above is the fact that the majority of the doctors in this country know little or nothing about the largest cause of illness in this country, *Stress*. Many physicians don't even believe in stress but rather see it as issues that are entirely in the head of the patient. Many doctors seem to believe that the patient's lifestyle and thoughts have absolutely nothing to do with his body. They see his thoughts and his beliefs as separate from the body. They are often totally unaware of the causes of illnesses their patients suffer from. In the end, the medical profession in its present form does nothing about this. The medical education process still teaches little if anything about stress, very little about nutrition and next to nothing about lifestyle. It is primarily involved in teaching young doctors that illness exists, how to recognize it and how to treat it. Causes other than biologic and genetic seem entirely unimportant.

Long ago I learned that if you are not part of the solution you must be part of the problem. Since the medical profession is uninterested in the real problems and the real causes of illness, only its effects, it too must be part of the problem of the creation of illness. In fact, and statistics bear this out, when one looks at the level of the quality of health care in this country it should be clear that the medical profession is a major part of the problem. If it is not creating the solution, **prevention** and **cure** of illness, then we must recognize that today's medical profession is *truly designed to keep people sick and get paid for it.* The present concept of medicine is now so deeply ingrained within the members of the medical profession that they can't even see it. In fact, it is possible that no amount of proof will convince them at this point. The U.S. is 16th in overall health care in the world, has one of the highest neonatal and infant death rates, has more malnutrition than many poor countries, has a high degree of death from problems that are almost entirely solvable such as heart disease and cancer and has a miserable record for treating such illnesses as diabetes, hypertension and autoimmune disease. Get a reference if possible. These facts say something about the ultimate beliefs of the medical profession and the way they have designed the medical care system.

The average general practitioner is so bogged down treating upper respiratory infections, colds and flues which are primarily viral and for the most part untreatable, that he has insufficient time to take care of, educate and work with the people who are really sick. Very often patients who have simple upper respiratory illnesses are given very potent and very dangerous antibiotics. Today patients often come to the doctors office and de-

mand antibiotics by name. Yet the medical profession has made no decisive move to educate the general public that *these illnesses should notbe
treated with antibiotics and that antibiotics can in fact be much more dangerous than the condition they are being used to treat.* Neither has there
been any education on how to prevent or treat these viral conditions at
home so that these practitioners are not bogged down. Both the general
practitioner and specialist alike are spending little time educating their patients and this reflects directly in the patients' lack of results and their
inability to cure themselves of illnesses and diseases that are entirely cur-
able.

Physicians as a whole are taught nothing about *true prevention.* In the
place of prevention they are taught about immunization which is only an
extremely small aspect of the preventive medicine armamentarium. Physicians are also not taught about *proper, wholesome nutrition.* Instead they
are taught about diseases of malnutrition which are common in third world
countries and poor rural areas of the U.S. but not in the suburban or urban
population they ultimately choose to serve. As we stated earlier physicians
are not taught about stress, nor are they taught about the interrelationship
of the mind, body and spirit. While they learn about the psyche, emotions
and mental illnesses, these subjects are often not integrated as issues of the
whole person but are taught separately as if they were entirely different
entities. Along with the lack of training in the areas listed above, today's
physician is not taught to recognize spiritual crises or spiritualemergencies.

For thousands of years the peoples of the world have been aware that a
major aspect of human existence is the process of spiritual transformation.
The process of this transformation or enlightenment, we are told, is ultimately essential for becoming a full and complete person. In most literature about this process of spiritual awakening we are told that it has physical, emotional and mental components. The medical profession has chosen
to ignore this information and instead lead the individual and the physical
conflicts he demonstrates during this process to the religious establishment.
Within Eastern medicine this concept is not only well recognized but it is
seen as a substantial issue that many, if not all people must go through. The
practitioners of Eastern philosophy recognize that if this process is frustrated or obstructed by poor handling of its physical and/or emotional components, it can result in harm to the patient. In Western Medicine this transformation is often seen either as mental illness or is missed entirely. Few
physicians are either interested or trained in understanding this area. Tens
of millions of persons with physical, emotional or mental symptoms directly attributable to this transformation process are blocked and stunted in
their development while their trusted medical doctors treat them for physi-

cal or mental ailments with potentially dangerous medications, oblivious to what is really happening. Our medical system, a product of 15th century mechanical thinking, refuses to acknowledge this process, to learn about it or to teach it. Hence, physicians not only can't recognize it but they are generally unaware that it even exists. The end result is that people who go to their family physician with the belief that he will help them, protect them from illness and cure them when they become ill aren't getting what they want or even what they are paying for. In fact, they are often misled and ultimately harmed by those they have trusted.

What can be done about this hurt is part of the mission of this book. We believe that introducing information about Huna is essential. Over thousands of years, Huna masters have developed a system which can identify the causes of illness and create solutions without the use of drugs and without harm to the patient. We will be discussing these possibilities throughout the second section of this book.

We have introduced Huna so that you can see the value of integrating this belief system or some system like it into our current medical practices in order to solve the problems that are causing great suffering to the peoples of the world. We also want to give you information about what you yourself can do about becoming well, preventing illness, getting off prescribed medication andpreventing unnecessary surgery. We do not propose that you leave the medical establishment, nor end your medical care. We want to show you how you can add to it a new dimension in healing, a new way of thinking which can help you maximize your ability to get well and lead a long and joyful life. *Using Huna does not require that you stop your current medical care, stop taking your medication or refuse planned or necessary surgery.* It would be unethical and quite imprudent for us to tell you to stop your medical treatment program. Huna is simply a way of thinking that allows you to better understand the integration of mind, body and spirit. When used correctly it can provide a number of easy to use healing techniques which will facilitate your present medical care program or act as a preventive health strategy. Huna can help you make your treatment program more effective and can speed up your healing. In fact, Huna can help you to ultimately heal your condition and possibly never need medications or drugs again.

CHAPTER TWO

MEDICINE AND ITS FUTURE

THE EFFECT OF THE PRESENT SYSTEM
ON ITS OWN MEMBERS

Earlier we suggested that the medical profession as a whole had fallen down on its job of getting people well. We stated that it is presently more about treatment than about cure and that many patients are dissatisfied with this situation. Patients want more time and more information while physicians are being forced to spend less time, charge more money and see more patients. We have discussed some of the more salient effects of this on the public and how it is affecting medical practice, but what about the physician and how is it affecting him?

The long term effects of the changes which have been occurring are indeed taking a toll on physicians, nurses and health care workers. Nurses are overworked, under paid and often feel frustrated with the level of patient care they see around them. Physicians are by no means immune to dissatisfaction. While many physicians are unaffected by the new pressures and changes and remain quite happy and satisfied with their role, others are not. Over the years, we have found that a great number of physicians we have come in contact with are unhappy, feeling empty and missing the purpose for which they originally went into medicine. Unfortunately, too often these physicians are not even aware that they are unhappy. However, their actions and lifestyles tell us what they are unable to find words to say.

It is our personal observation that the physicians who are quite happy and fulfilled represent only a small percentage of physicians. We believe that a far greater number of physicians are indeed quite unhappy and disappointed in American medicine. While it is probably obvious to most physicians that medicine doesn't give them what they originally wanted which was to heal people, many now find themselves in it merely for the money as nothing else gives satisfaction. There is an extremely high rate of alcoholism, drug addiction, suicide, depression, family problems and divorce among today's physicians. They are not doing what they want and they are not being what they want to be. This not only creates illness in themselves, but until they can solve their own problems, they are going to be much less effective in curing their patients. Some physicians are leaving medicine looking for new opportunities to feel useful. Others use thepractice of medicine to "mine" their patients so that they can invest in business. Many are no longer emotionally invested in either their patients or the practice of medicine. Still others simply tolerate it, slowly dying inside and eventually ending up with chronic diseases, heart disease or cancers themselves. The culprit in all of this is not the physician but the medical system as it has evolved from Newton and Descartes forward over the past 500 years. Just as physicists have found that Newtonian physics is only valuable to a certain point, it is rapidly becoming clear that Newtonian-Cartesian science and hence medicine is also only good to a certain point. The reliance on pure science without a heart or a soul is conducive to illness. Fritjov Capra in his book *The Turning Point* suggests that there is a new paradigm of health care on the horizon. We clearly see signs of this all over. The question, however, is, will we see a system that is involved in healing or one which is invested even more in technology?

What Huna has to offer to the physician as well as to the general public is a new way of looking at the interrelation of mind, body and spirit in creating wellness and prevention of illness.

TREATMENT VERSUS CURE

Possibly the largest problem with the medical profession today is the fact that they are moredirected at treating than curing. In our earlier discussion we touched on this briefly. However, it is of such great importance that it needs a broader examination. While many physicians talk about cures and cure rates most physicians are comfortable with simply treating the patient. In a sense it is bad business for the medical profession to cure a patient for when he is cured, he stops coming to the physician.

The patient says he wants to get *well*, however, he wants to do this with as little work as is possible on his part. The general public knows that the American diet is poor, deficient in vitamins and minerals, overloaded with salt and sugar but he chooses to do nothing about it and to ignore warnings as long as possible. For many, taking medications or having surgery is often the easiest way to deal with their problems. There is an old saying which sums it up, "when you have done something wrong you ought to take your medicine and then get on with your life." The problems of inadequate and unhealthy foods, air pollution, stress and never ending materialism is so large that one can think of it as a kind of conspiracy between many members of the medical profession, the food industry and American business. Everyone knows we are damaging the health of our society, our children and our planet but no one (certainly not the medical professions, the guardians of public health) are willing to stand up and do anything about it.

There is also a conspiracy that exists between the patients and their physicians. The physician won't ask the patients about their problems, the things that are really bothering them, the stresses in their life, their fears and their feelings of guilt and shame. The patients then won't have to face themselves and look at the lies, faulty beliefs and conflicts they have created for themselves. In this way the patient doesn't have to experience the pain of looking at his life and the physician won't have to cure him. Through this conspiracy, both sides get what they want. The patient feels no pain and the physician never has to lose his patient. The patient gradually gets sicker which often works for him as he gets to pay his dues for his feelings of worthlessness; and makes retribution for the sins he feels guilty about. He continues to experience fear of living in a Universe that is home and yet foreign to him. The physician accepts this, turning his head and choosing not to see it. He collects his fees and feels so empty he has to turn to worshiping basketball, football and baseball players. He buys himself a bigger home, a grander car and still underneath secretly wonders why something is missing in his life. Unfortunately, the physician is also a person and eventually his lies and guilt catch up with him and he too falls ill. The end result is that the problems that cause their illnesses are neither found nor defined. The doctor misses his opportunity to cure his patient. At the same time, of course, the patient misses his opportunity to be cured.

It is this conspiracy of silence that takes the doctor away from being a healer and puts him into the realm of a sophisticated technician. As the physician begins to understand Huna and the process of illness, how it works and how illnesses occur, he will eventually understand how to return to the role of the healer. When he uses Huna as a part of caring for his patient he becomes the healer and also has the opportunity to heal himself.

With fewer sick people to attend to the physician will have the opportunity to spend more time with those who need it. As there is less illness the physician will have more time to educate and enlighten himself.

THE ROLE OF THE PRACTICING PHYSICIAN

Until recent years the role of the physician has been to guide and manage the medical care of the individual who was sick. The physician, however, played little if any role in managing or helping the patient to maintain his or her wellness and good health. The physician, for the most part, was singularly responsible for the medical and health education of his patient. If he did his job well, his patients were able to make healthier choices and better decisions regarding their health care. If he didn't do his job well the patient often suffered for the lack of information and ability to make healthful decisions.

In more recent years a good part of this role has been taken from the personal physician by the newspaper, magazine, radio and television media as well as books written by other doctors. Some of these book advise their readers about what is right and wrong and how to be careful and aware of the inadequacies and problems of the medical profession. Others like this introduce new ideas from old cultures. Some of the ideas they present are useful while others ask the reader to do things that do not usually fit into the reader's lifestyle.

Fifty years ago the primary physician was the family doctor. In recent years there has been a swing toward specialists. Today the discussion is how to get physicians to return to being the basic care provider, the family doctor. While this swing back to the desirability of having the physician as a primary care giver has much to do with economics, we suggest another reason. The public is not getting what they want. Results are not forthcoming from the medical community. Lastly, many physicians left the practice of primary medicine because they were not getting their patients better. Many of these physicians believed that as primary care practitioners they didn't know enough and if they became a specialist their situation would get better. For some physicians professional life did get better but for most nothing changed, they still found themselves unable to get the results they wanted.

Today the role of the practicing physician is rapidly changing. He is making fewer decisions for his patient, and he is required to get more and more outside (bureaucratic) permission to fully takecare of his patient. This is not by accident, nor because of economics. The physicians of this country have demonstrated they are more involved in their own egos and personal interest than they are in the needs of their patients. The loss of credibility of the medical profession is, in a sense, a punishment for their unwillingness to reduce illness, long term care and chronic, debilitating disease. The evidence for this conclusion is demonstrated by the massive movement of people who are sick away from the medical profession and toward alternative sources of health care services, such as chiropractic, acupuncture, nutritionists, etc.. People are dissatisfied with the medical profession as it now operates because they want to get well and the medical profession is not helping them to do this.

Tomorrow's physician may have less and less responsibility and even more of a role in performing paperwork to assist his patient in obtaining proper care. If changes are not made soon the already troubled health care system will become a disaster. As things are presently going it appears that within the next few years more and more health care decisions will be in the hands of clerks and bureaucrats of the insurance companies. In many cases non-medical people are making important, life threatening decisions. Often the patient's physician is bypassed entirely having no say in what the insurance company or governmental agency decides. Decisions about patient care is made by people who have never seen the patient, never touched nor examined the patient. While the insurance companies tell us that this is necessary to reduce the cost of medical care, the truth is that more attention is paid to the containment of costs then to quality of care. Ultimately, then, insurance companies are practicing medicine and directing treatment. In the end, the patient gets substandard care and the physician is being relegated to the role of a skilled technician.

The question that eventually comes up for many is, "Who is to blame and what is the problem?" The answer is we are all to blame. Doctors, nurses, insurance companies, the government and the consumer. The primary problem is our need to define whether medicine is a business or a right of the people. The secondary problem is for the medical profession to decide whether the role of the physician and the medical system is to provide a significant income for its members or to take care of the health and well-being of the public.

Lastly, the public must decide whether they want to have care under the control of the physician they choose and who cares about them or directed by insurance companies and governmental bureaucracies. The solution to all of these questions is that we must get past our egos and create a system that provides a decent living for the medical practitioners yet integrates into the health system the wisdom and learning of the ages, the systems of healing which are directed at getting people well, preventing future illness and which are affordable for everyone.

Physicians are administered the Hippocratic oath upon graduation from medical school yet many forget what they are supposed to be doing. Many physicians unfortunately forget the needs of the patient and place their egos, biases and prejudices above the welfare of their patients. And they often do this in the name of science. The role of the practicing physician must be to protect the physical, mental, emotional and *spiritual* well-being of his patient. To evaluate, recognize and defeat *all* illnesses whether of a physical, mental, emotional or spiritual nature. The role of the physician is to educate, inform, prevent and protect his or her patient not just when they are sick but before they get sick so that they do not have to become sick. We have not done this as a profession and this must be done if we are to survive and the public is to get the absolute best health care system available.

To this end we introduce to the medical profession and the general public a system that provides adimension that has previously been entirely left out of health care. It is our belief that the integration of this system and others like it will reduce and prevent untold suffering in the future. In the next sections we will provide not only an overview of Huna as it was practiced but we will also suggest ways in which it fits into the current system. We believe that it can change the present system in a very positive direction and that it will add to the system in such a way as to make it richer and more successful than ever. The overall goal of this work is to stimulate and promote healing and reduce unnecessary illness.

SECTION II

HUNA, AN
ANCIENT HEALING ART

CHAPTER ONE

The Art of Huna Medicine, Ancient and New

WHAT IS HUNA?

Huna in Hawaiian means *the Secret*. The origins of Huna are not very clear. According to Max Freedom Long, the pioneer investigator and researcher of Huna who once called himself the *Recoverer of Huna*, Huna has been traced back to the time of the building of the great pyramids of ancient Egypt. It is possible, however, that it has existed in one form or another for many thousands of years even before this. Evidence suggests that it might be traced to the occult *mysteries* of the ancient world. Little is known about these ancient mysteries except that they are the basis of all of today's spiritual and religious teachings. Huna may well represent a living example of the mysteries which, because of the isolation of the Polynesian and Hawaiian peoples, have survived in their original form to the present day. Whatever its origin, it is as relevant today as it was thousands of years ago.

THE SECRET OF HUNA

The Huna masters feared that Huna was so powerful that it could cause as much harm as good if used incorrectly. They believed that this special knowledge must be withheld from the masses to keep it from being used for profane or evil purposes or from becoming mundane. They, therefore, buried the secret of Huna within the common everyday language of the people so it could be recognized on a daily basis by those who understood its keys. Only those persons chosen by a Huna master and indoctrinated carefully by him (or her) could be given the secret. By maintaining the body of knowledge of Huna in this fashion, it was kept in a safe place while being passed on whole and complete from generation to generation, right under everybody's eyes.

In the late 1860's when the missionaries came to Hawaii there were many *Kahuna* trained in the art of healing. The missionaries, however, saw their own Christian way of doing things as the only way. As soon as they gained sufficient power to control the people of Hawaii they began to outlaw this "native magic." Strangely enough, the missionaries who brought Christ to the Hawaiians were welcomed with open arms. Christianity as told to the Hawaiians was readily accepted for it was immediately clear to the Hawaiians that Jesus was *a great Kahuna and understood Huna.* The words of Jesus, his parables and metaphors *were* Huna. However, within a short time the Hawaiians became somewhat disillusioned with the missionaries and the other westerners who lived in Hawaii when they saw that most of them neither lived the principles of Christianity nor really understood what Christianity was all about.

For the Hawaiians giving power (mana) to their prayers was essential. The Christians, however, simply said their prayers and then they would get up and leave the church. The Hawaiians named the westerners, *haule's,* meaning *breathless ones* because the westerners used no *mana* or energy of the lower self to send their prayer to the Higher Self (Jesus or God). As the missionaries gave no breath (power) to their prayers and sent no gift of mana up to their Lord to prove their love and desire, the Hawaiians couldn't understand how their Aumakua, Jesus, could grant them what they wanted. While the Hawaiians could immediately see the similarities between their system of beliefs and Christianity, the missionaries could not. Feeling threatened by the *savage beliefs* of the Hawaiians, they outlawed the right of the Hawaiians to maintain their beliefs in their own land. In much the same way missionaries and Americans of European ancestry had invaded the ancestral lands of theAmerican Indians, stole their lands and undermined their Gods, their beliefs and their civilizations under the pretext of saving their souls.

From the late 1800's until the 1950's Huna remained illegal and its practitioners, if discovered, were sent to jail. By the time these suppressive laws were reversed, Huna had all but disappeared. Very few new Kahunas were being trained and what training did persist did so in great secrecy. Because the whole-hearted acceptance of Christianity by a large portion of the Hawaiian people and the fact that old Huna masters had died, a good deal of the knowledge of Huna was lost. Fortunately, however, the key to Huna, hidden in the Hawaiian language, remained intact. In the 1930's a haule school teacher, Max Freedom Long, teaching on Molokai, became fascinated by the stories of ancient Hawaiian healing that he would hear, from time to time, when the Hawaiians talked. Enthralled by these stories, he set out on a life quest to rediscover the Secrets of Huna. In a number of volummes of books he describes his journey and what he found.

Today while many of the elements of Huna have been rediscovered and introduced to the world at large, some key elements still remain buried with the ancient ones. However, enough has been brought to light to begin the process of healing the world.

HUNA AND THE MODERN WORLD

What do the ancient secrets of Huna have to offer modern science? Huna represents a new and valuable way of looking at the interrelationship of man and his body, his mind and his spiritual nature. While present day scientists and physicians rely on the old Cartesian- Newtonian view of man as a machine, Huna sees man much more along the lines of the new scientific paradigm and Quantum physics. In the Cartesian-Newtonian viewpoint, that has been the basis of Western medical tradition, the body and mind are one-dimensional. They exist only on a physical-mechanical-biologic plane. In this context we can look at the anatomy, physiology or biochemistry of man but we cannot wholly interrelate these with the concept of life itself or with the spiritual aspects of man. Medical students learn about medicine from books and about patient care from dealing with people who are sick. However, they often have great difficulties seeing their patients as people with stresses, faulty beliefs, failed aspirations and human flaws. Occasionally, some physicians can create a two dimensional view of man as a body and a mind but the third aspect, the spiritual aspect, is often extremely difficult or even impossible for him to understand. Instead, he commonly substitutes his own religious perspective. Unfortunately, he frequently believes that religion and the spiritual aspects of man are the same thing.

Several concepts which are well understood by so called primitive societies are virtuallynon-existent in Western medicine. For example, death, the transitions of birth and death, reincarnation, the spirit world and the soul, life after death, the energies of the life force and our connection to the Intelligence of the Universe (God, if you wish). Without understandings of these concepts the physician really cannot heal the sick nor prevent illness. He can merely treat, remove or fix broken parts but he cannot heal the problems which cause his patient's illness.

The Huna concept of sickness is much different from the Western idea of sickness. As a physician and as a counsellor we would like to believe that we have the better system, that we are able to heal much, if not all, of the illnesses we see. However, this is simply not true. The record of the medical profession is, in fact, dismal. While we can heal some conditions that affect mankind, our "science" doesn't provide us with sufficient understanding or information to heal the majority of problems. Instead we *treat* people. In many cases we treat our patients throughout their entire lifetime. Can we really call this a cure-oriented system? The concept of treatment has so taken over the construct of cure that Western physicians cannot tell the difference between them. In fact, medical people often become belligerent when one tries to suggest that there is indeed a difference between treatment and cure.

For the Huna master, illness is entirely different. It is caused not by bacteria or germs but rather by faulty beliefs, evil thoughts and by the sins he has committed by intentionally causing harm to others for which he has not made amends. Illness can occur from possession by disembodied spirits and by lack of self love. The Huna master knows that these "evils" are the cause of illness and that their resolution and elimination is what is necessary to "cure" the illness and set everything right once again. When he works with his patient he works to uncover these problems and to assist the patient in making amends for his sins. He encourages the patient to be of service to his community and to take better care of himself through feeling better about himself.

Another problem of the Western system is its willingness to blame the messenger for the message. When the physician is unable to heal a patient, he often blames the patient for being uncooperative. If the condition seems to be one caused by stress or conflict of ideation, the physician often labels his problems as *psychosomatic* or tell the patient or his family that his illness is *all in his head*. When a condition does not respond to the physician's treatment (that is, exactly the way he wants it to by his criteria) he often tells the patient that the condition is *incurable* or refers him to a specialist *because a specialist has more experience with the specific condition.*

The Huna oriented physician recognizes that he has the power to cast a spell over his patient to heal him and, in certain cases, he does just this. However, the Huna master also recognizes that resolution and healing is best established when the patient finds his own way to solve his problems. To support this the Huna master knows that his best help is to act as a guide and not take the responsibility away from his patient. The Huna oriented physician knows that there is no higher source for healing than the patient's own self and his resource is his Higher Self. When medical treatment doesn't work and all has seemed to fail, the Western physician often turns to the family and says, "It is now in God's hands. I suggest you pray." The Huna oriented physician almost always operates through prayer, not seeing it as a last resort but rather as a primary tool which both he and his patient can use to reconstruct what has gone wrong, solve problems and create a new and healthy future.

Another conflict is that Western medicine is based on scientific research. If a problem does not bear out in research it is either ignored or thrown out as unproductive. Laboratory tests have to agree with known patterns and when they don't many physicians lose interest. Things that do not easily lend themselves to medical research are often ignored or categorized as *not understandableat this time*. Illnesses are not allowed to have a spiritual component. The physician treats only the medical aspect and refers the patient to a priest, rabbi or minister to deal with the spiritual aspects.

For the Huna master all problems are spiritual and have a spiritual component. He cannot conceive of man without a spirit no more than he can conceive of living without a head. He needs no laboratory test for he knows that we are connected to the intelligence of the Universe. When answers are needed, one only has to ask for answers and then wait for them to come. His science is the interaction of the mind, body and spirit. The Huna master did not write. Nothing needed to be written down. Life was not so complex so there was no need to be intimidated by it. He was medicine man and spiritualist; he was physician and friend; he was healer and confessor. What the Huna master understood was learned over generations. It was passed on through practical hands on day-to-day working and one-to-one training and not through books. All he needed to know existed within his heart and soul. He was a healer. This was a trust, one which he not only took seriously but addressed with confidence and love.

The fractionalization of western health care services leaves many people permanently sick. They are in a nowhere zone between a medical profession limited by their own books and laws and non-medical, alternative systems which traditional physicians ridicule and deride. The medicalprofession tells the public that alternative medicine is practiced by charlatans and hence should be avoided. In doing this they create an even greater breach between the medical community and those who are sick. To understand Huna one must think differently. One must learn to give up linear and one-dimensional thinking. As with Quantum physics, one has to think in four dimensions, that of body, mind, spirit and the energy that makes it all work. The purpose of this work is to outline for the reader the comparisons and contrasts of two different healing systems. These are the Interventive Medical

System (our name for the present medical system which basically says, "If you get broken we can fix you.") and the Healing Medical System where each person is seen as a living spiritual being in an Intelligent Universe.

It is our belief that these systems can, by taking their best attributes, be integrated. This process will not eliminate the Interventive Medical System but add another important and extremely valuable dimension to it. This Integrated System will say, "Come to us before you get sick and we will help you to prevent suffering illness. We will show you that illness is an Intelligent act of the body and together we will find the conflicts and problems that disturb your harmony and balance and then you and I, working together, will heal them."

HUNA AND RELIGION

There are remarkable similarities between Huna and both ancient Christianity and Eastern spiritual healing beliefs. Not unlike the secret code that underlies the Bible, Huna is embedded in the language of the Polynesian and Hawaiian peoples. Huna, in its truest sense, is not a religion but rather a form of psychology which integrates the workings of the physical body with the structure of the mind and the spiritual nature of the individual. Unlike Western medicine, Huna involves the *whole person* in the creation of both illness and wellness. The basic fabric of Huna is the recognition that man is integral with the Universe and that what he believes and how he acts affects not only his own outcome but also the structure of the world around him. In Huna to be healthy one must integrate all together within himself and within his environment, the three integral parts of himself, the *lower self* or subconscious, *the middle self* or conscious self and the *Higher Self* or spiritual connection to the Universe. We will discuss these three selves in much greater detail in a later section of this book.

As we said earlier, Huna differs, in a number of significant ways, from the Newtonian-Cartesian based Western medicine with which we are most familiar. While Huna does recognize that illness exists and the Huna master does not consider it to be a condition caused by something outside of us (such as bacteria, viruses and parasites.) but rather as occurring from within us related to the way we think and what we believe about ourselves. Unlike Western thinking which long agoseparated medicine and religion, Huna remained integrated. Huna, however, is not a religion because it has no dogma. It doesn't even have a view of God. The founders of Huna believed that God was so far above them that there was no sense in either worrying about a deity or praying to it. The Huna master believed that God has no interest in our day-to-day life. Instead, the Huna masters created a system which was ideal for our simple lifestyle; one which gives answers rather than creates problems as to the nature and loyalty of the God head. The ancient believer in Huna saw himself as being made up of a powerful human intelligence yet still having an animalistic nature. He saw this animal part of himself not as a burden nor an enemy but rather as a loving creature that ceaselessly took care of all of his bodily needs and functions. He called this aspect *the low self*, according to Max Freedom Long. We prefer to call it *the lower self* and will use this name throughout the remainder of this book. Finally, the Huna master, unlike the physicians of Western medicine and priests of Western religions, believed that there was *one and only one sin*, the intentional infliction of hurt upon another (which we believe includes the intentional infliction of harm upon yourself).

Huna, therefore, could be described as the science of the integration of mind, body and spirit. It provides an extremely valuable way of understanding the holism of the person. Healing through Huna is based on our ability to integrate all of these aspects into a oneness of being. Huna heals through the harmonization of thought, mind, body and spirit. While modern medical philosophy denies what it can't see, Huna uses what can't be seen to create changes to heal. Underlying the basis of Huna is that it recognizes that the body is formed and structured from energy. By using an understanding of the nature of the Universe, which we presently recognize as the laws of Newtonian and quantum physics combined, the Huna masters created a set of natural techniques to transform the energy of illness into the energy of wellness. Unlike medicine, Huna recognizes that distortion of energy, negative thoughts and faulty beliefs, can create illness. It recognizes that the mind has both the power to create illness and to heal it. Huna also suggests that illness is ultimately the result of our own faulty thoughts, deeds and actions which subvert our body. Recently, Western science-based researchers have demonstrated this phenomena showing that there are both positive and negative effects on the immune system created simply by what people believe.

While our language has not intentionally been infused with the secret knowledge of the ages, it has embedded within it an enormous amount of wisdom. In fact, as I wrote in my book *BodySymptom Language©*, what we think, how we talk, what we say and especially what we believe are extremely important factors in the control and creation of both our wellness and our illnesses. To understand this it would be helpful to see how the Hawaiians used their language. Then we will briefly discuss how we, in our society today, use our language to affect wellness and well-being.

The Hawaiian language is made up of a series of root words which, when added to other root words, create virtually an infinite language. For example, the Hawaiian word for "life" is *ola*. This word translates from two root words "o" and "la." "O"means "belonging to" and "la" means "light." Hence, in Hawaiian the word life would be translated as "belonging to the light." Here the word "light" refers to daylight but it also symbolizes the construct of human consciousness. Notice from this very simple example how Huna begins to be embedded in the language. If we were to interpret the word "light" from the Western Christian sense it might suggest truth, or even God (as in, "I am the Light") or Intelligence. Hence, "belonging to the light" might suggest, belonging to the truth, belonging to God or belonging to the Intelligence of the Universe. In a similar way "La-a" is the Higher "light" and in ordinary translation would mean "sacred." Unfortunately the purpose of this work does not allow us to go deeply into the linguistic aspects of Huna. For those interested we have provided a large bibliography of titles that delve considerably more deeply into this aspect.

THE PURPOSE OF HUNA

There appears to be little doubt the people who designed the system underlying Huna meant it as a system of healing and preventive health. We believe that this is true of the Bible as well. When we look closely at the Bible, past the religious dogma and the sales literature of the religion, we see that both the Old Testament and the New Testament are really textbooks of healing and wellness. Certainly, few people could argue that, if we followed all of the Ten Commandments and the instructions on how to live our life, the chances of physical, mental, emotional and spiritual illness would be greatly diminished. However, Huna remained predominantly as it was designed while the Bible was ultimately transformed into a body of religious dogma.

As we stated earlier, the power of Huna ultimately lies in its ability to help us understand how the human mind, body and spirit all work together to maintain wellness and health. It also provides an opportunity to understand how poor integration or breakdown of this triad of the Self can lead to illness and disease. Through understanding Huna and its view of man, one can see how its doctrine, recognizing only one sin, can affect the structure of society. It creates a system which can virtually be entirely free of guilt, shame, confusion and fear; all of the conditions that commonly lead to illness and disease. Since Huna provides us with a way of looking at death and the spirit world, it can give us a true sense of spiritual connection to the Universe and our mortality. Western medicine and religion have no all-inclusive system which allows us to integrate our physical, emotional and spiritual selves into both the material world and spiritual worlds which surround us. Organized medicine encompasses neither an environmental or spiritual view. The modern physician expects the individual's *religious beliefs or dogma* to provide him his world view. When this doesn't happen or his view is faulty, the physician is often powerless to help the patient integrate his life to cure his illness or assist him in dealing with his own mortality.

HOW IS HUNA USED?

The practitioners of Huna, while technically shaman, were for the most part the equivalent of today's practitioners of medicine, psychiatry and psychology. They were generally, in terms of their society, highly educated men and women. The Kahuna or keeper of the secret were found in a multitude of fields besides healing. For example, there were Kahuna in such areas as agriculture, weather, oceanography, canoe making, sailing, law and the military. If an individual had a problem in a specific area of his life he would seek out a Kahuna in that field. If an individual had an injury or health, psychological or emotional problems he would most commonly seek out a Kahuna who specialized in psychology, herbology, physical medicine (lomi-lomi) or in the spiritual realm. Within the group of Kahunas that dealt with health and illnessthere were many levels, not unlike our present medical system. There were lay practitioners, general practitioners, specialists and teachers.

The Huna master was a trained specialist. Each master taught his craft to one or more students whom he chose at the time of their birth. The student was often taken from his family to live in the house of the Huna master, to grow up watching and learning what the Huna master had to teach. No child was chosen unless the Huna masters could see certain signs that he was indeed a healer. At the highest levels, the Huna masters were extremely powerful people. The secrets of Huna allowed them to perform many feats which would be considered by modern standards to be either impossible or unbelievable. When the Huna master was skilled enough to make full contact with his Higher Self he could perform instant healing. In one recorded case a guest on his way to visit a Huna master fell and broke his leg just outside of the master's house. Several of the towns people had examined the leg and agreed that it was badly broken. The bone was pushing up under the skin. When the Huna master arrived, she took hold of the guests leg, prayed for a short period of time and then told the guest to rise. The guest was able to get up and walk, without a limp as if nothing had happened. So powerful were Huna masters that they were able to raise the dead, heal incurable diseases,control the weather, foretell the future and create military victories. It is even said that certain masters were able to communicate with sharks causing them not to eat local natives while swimming around the Hawaiian Islands.

These stories have been recorded over many years and substantiated by many credible witnesses. While these claims may sound incredible, the Hawaiian Kahuna were not the only ones who could perform such miracles. The Bible is filled with stories of Jesus performing exactly the same kinds of miracles. According to Long, as we mentioned earlier, Jesus was a Huna master. If you believe that, what Jesus did was different because he was the Son of God, you must understand two things. In Huna all people are recognized as the Sons of God. When the Huna master refers to the concept of the Son of God he is generally referring to the concept that we are all connected by our Higher Self to God. Long points out that what Jesus was saying was entirely Huna in nature for he was defining the relationship which we all have with our Higher Self. Finally, as far as the ability of the Huna master to perform *miracles*, when Jesus spoke to his disciples he told them, "Truly, truly, I say to you, he who believes in Me, the works that I do shall he do also, and greater works than these *shall he* do."

While it may appear that the healing-preventive health system of the Hawaiians occurred when the sick person or a member of the family would seek out the Huna master, in actually started long before that. The Hawaiian society (unlike our own) was structured to prevent illness. Life was extremely simple; there was little stress. To help eliminate stress, a series of Taboos (somewhat like our own Ten Commandments) were set up. The people worked together for a common goal. There were many rituals and prayers that were used to heal, reduce or eliminate stress. While the Hawaiians, like all other people, exhibited jealousy and frustration, the structure of their society was designed to minimize it.

The practitioner of Huna understood the psychology of the people as well as the underlying causes of illness and disease and their cures. While the Huna master was not advanced in the sense of modern medical theory, he was considerably more sophisticated in the understanding of the dynamics of the body, the mind and the spirit. Even though he had never heard of micro-organisms such as bacteria and viruses, he understood their essence. He referred to ideas, beliefs, complexes and spirits which caused illness as *eating creatures or eating partners*. The Huna master saw the causes of illness and disease differently from the way the modern physician who sees micro-organisms. The Huna master recognized these invaders which if allowed into the body by our actions, beliefs and behaviors, could infect it and ultimately destroyit. Although the Huna master acknowledged the power of these eating creatures, he also acknowledged the power of the mind to destroy them or throw them out. He recognized them as powerful adversaries and he knew that they had to be eliminated in order for the individual to return to health and well-being.

Unlike the modern Western physician, the Huna master believed in spirits. He considered one of the sources of these eating creatures to be disembodied spirits. He recognized that these spirits had the power to invade and take over a body when it was vulnerable, ill or in disharmony with itself or the world around it. He believed these disembodied spirits were actually aspects of the lower or middle self which, after death, had not moved on to the after-world. The Huna master believed that thoughts were real and material "things." Each thought had a kind of power of its own. He called them *thought forms*. Once born, these thought forms often shaped our life. They could change our direction, change the way we lived our life and change the world around us. Our "thoughts" remain attached to us all through our life, dropping away only when we replace our old thought with new and more powerful thoughts or when the thought is no longer important to us. He realized, however, that just because we lost track of our thoughts or let them out of our consciousness, they were by no means gone. While out of sight or out of mind, our thoughts stillhad power over us. They could continue to affect our life and they could even be responsible for our illnesses.

In the next sections we will look more directly at the three selves, the eating companions and thought forms. We will interpose these ideas with concepts of modern medicine and with the concepts of the newest and most sophisticated field in medicine, psychoneuroimmunobiology. We will look at stress as you have never seen it before and we will begin to show the true wisdom of Huna in action.

CHAPTER TWO

The Three Selves

The well trained physician learns a great deal about the human body. Medical school provides him with a course of study which includes a multitude of subjects including anatomy, biology, biochemistry, endocrinology, physiology, pathology, psychology, psychiatry, bacteriology and much more. However, it is generally left up to the student to integrate all of these disciplines into a process he can deal with in relations to the life and well-being of his patients. Generally, with all of the courses he takes, he is taught nothing about the *heart of man* except for the four chambered, 60-80 beat-per-minute variety which pumps blood through the arteries and veins of the body. He is given no information about the higher levels of consciousness of men. In the end, he views the body as exactly what the Newtonian-Cartesian model offers, a living machine disassociated from its thoughts, its environment and the remainder of its Universe.

The concept of the three selves defines man not as a multitude of parts or tissues but rather as aliving being functioning in three levels of consciousness. This organization doesn't replace the hierarchy taught in medical school but rather it adds to it another living dimension. No longer are organs simply factories and tissue with complex functions. Now we have a symphony of tissues, organs and structures each dependent on each other's intelligence; each part of a whole being and each part of the Intelligence of the Universe. Huna is a healing "science." Its ability to work is based on the ancient secret wisdom of the Huna masters. The Huna masters recognized that to heal one's self or others it was necessary to fully understand the three selves or the *three spirits* as they were sometimes called. The three selves are the essence of who we are as a person. Our knowledge of our three selves, the middle self, the lower self and the Higher Self is ultimately what determines our ability to heal ourselves as well as to live in harmony and optimal health. We might ask, "What do the three selves have to do with the practice of medicine?" The physician might further question, "What do the three selves have to do with the way I currently treat my patients?" The answers to both of these questions are extremely important to us if we want to get well or help other people get well.

The Western medical system only recognizes the conscious and aware state, the middle self. Thelevels of consciousness below the conscious level are often thought of as unimportant, even superfluous. Only the field of psychiatry ever gets involved in the realm of the unconscious. While physicians do talk about unconscious fears or unconscious motivations, most physicians rarely get involved with anything other than the physical body, its organs and biochemistry. If we as human beings were only a physical body, organs and biochemistry, this would be fine. In this situation simply understanding the internal workings of the body and its organs, not unlike working on an automobile, could allow a physician to fix virtually any problem. However, we are much more complex. In order to heal people, that is, help them get well and stay well, we must understand their more intricate levels, how they work and what they do. This is what the three selves are about.

People are not made up of just their physical bodies and organs. People are also thoughts and feelings, beliefs and desires. They are spiritual, emotional and mystical. While physicians trained within the Western medicine tradition have chosen to limit themselves to the territory of the physical body, the Huna practitioner would embrace the whole being, the physical, conscious, unconscious and spiritual aspects of the individual. When we talk about the three selves as if they are each separate entities, it is only a mechanism weuse to allow us to discuss the role of each component of the whole. The three selves cannot be separated from each other. They are each facets of the total person. They can, however, be out of synchrony with each other. In fact, it is this imbalance between them that we call disease that creates the opportunity for illness to occur.

In our society we generally consider it the role of the physician to attend to people who are sick. In fact, we usually expect them to heal and protect us. We even insist on it; yet this is not always the case. More often the physician sees his role as a *treater* and not a *healer*. While he may use the words "cure" and "heal" he generally doesn't perform this function. For example, a patient with high blood pressure is rarely cured but rather is put on long term treatment and, at best, controlled. A person with anxiety or panic reactions is more likely to be treated with medication by the physician than cured of the problems which caused the anxiety or panic in the first place. The same is probably true for maturity onset diabetes, peptic ulcer disease, ileitis, colitis, asthma, allergies and many other common medical problems. When the physician does talk of cure he frequently refers to it in terms of a surgical cure, of radiation therapy or chemotherapy for major illnesses or the use of antibiotics for bacterial infections. For the modern physician, "cure" generally means treatment of the symptoms of the illness for the rest of his patient's life or for relatively long periods of time.

THE SEVEN COMPONENTS OF THE INDIVIDUAL

According to Huna, there are a total of seven important components that make up each individual. The first three we will discuss in relatively great detail. The others, while important, will be discussed only briefly. It is not that these other four are not important but rather that they play a lesser role in creation or prevention of illness and are more involved with other aspects of life. The first three groups are the Lower Self (the subconscious mind), the Middle Self (the conscious mind) and the Higher Self (the superconscious).

In Huna, the fourth constituent is the soul. The soul is recognized as the essence of our being, our personal identity and our awareness of being aware. While the Huna master recognized it, he also considered it have no specific function. He believed that it could not be influenced or affected by us. Therefore, he put little effort into thinking about it or discussing it. For our purposes, we will just recognize that it exists and since it has no specific affect on creating wellness or eliminating illness, we will also not further involve ourselves with it.

The fifth member is the *aka body* or more accurately our *aka bodies*. Each of the levels of consciousness we have described has an aka body or astral or etheric bodies. These are probably the most difficult concepts for Westerners to grasp as there is nothing in our society that specifically relates to them. Some readers have undoubtedly read about *Kerlian Photography* or *auras*. Undoubtedly Kerlian photography measures the aka body of either the middle or lower self or both. When seen as a color or "energy field" around the body it is frequently called an aura. Some aura readers can see only one of these bodies while others can see all three. The halos often seen in religious art usually represent the aka body of the Higher Self which sits outside of the body and either above or to one side or the other of the head. The aka bodies generally act as one structure and are often referred to simply as the *aka body*. It completely interpenetrates the entire physical body, enveloping it completely. The aka body is extremely sensitive to thoughts and emotions changing in shape, size and color as they change. Possibly its most important consideration is that it contains the pattern of every cell, tissue and organ of the body. In the situation discussed earlier where the guest fell on his way to see the Kahuna and broke his leg, the Kahuna was able to repair the leg rapidly, not because she used magic but because she communicated with the wisdom of the body. She was able to communicate with the man's Higher Self and have it dissolve the injury (as bone and tissues are only made of energy) and reconstruct them according to the tissue cellular pattern (blueprint) which already existed in the aka body. When we hold faulty, distorted beliefs and thoughts for a long time, the blueprint of the bodywithin the aka body can be distorted. Disease and illness are the consequence. We can heal disease and illness, as we shall describe later, by using the energy of the Higher Self to reestablish healthy body patterns. Huna masters believe that everything we come in contact with throughout our life becomes attached to our aka body. This allows us to have what appears to the uninitiated to be psychic powers. According to this concept we can *know* things about objects we touch or people we meet because we can communicate through our aka body and its connections to the aka bodies of others. The aka is sticky so that when we touch, shake hands or even look at others we develop a connection with them. The more we have touched or been in contact, the stronger the bond. We have all heard stories of a mother, sister or brother who suddenly realized a family member is in trouble. The concept of the aka connection makes it easy not only to see how this can happen but also to learn how to do this. We believe that we all spring from an infinite Intelligent Universe. This Universe is made up of a special energy, *Intelligent Energy* or simply, *The Intelligence*. The Huna master would say that this Intelligent Energy is the aka of the universe.

The sixth component we will discuss in great detail in later chapters is the *mana* or energy of the individual. This energy or life force exists as a product of life. When life leaves (when we die) this energy dissipates. While it comes out of the Intelligent Universe it is not in itself the Intelligence. It is used by the Intelligence to animate, to create opportunity for things to happen and the means to make them happen. Yet it is not only these components of the energy force and it takes all of them working together for it to be effective. A practitioner uses mana in the process of healing, which means he uses mentally directed energy, confidence, authority and skill. This is his *"power."*[3] Perhaps you can see now how effective the relationship of Huna to the practice of medicine can be. The physician who uses his medical skill *along with* mentally directed energy, knowing the makeup of not only the physical body but the Huna concept of the body, can significantly increase his "power" to heal. No longer does he need only treat; he can now use the power he gains through this ancient healing wisdom to empower his ability to heal his patients of the problems which cause their illnesses.

The last of the seven components is the *physical body*. In Hawaiian, the physical body is referred to as the *kino*. Kino essentially means *a highly energized thought form*. Serge King, a Kahuna,writes, "In Huna teaching, your body is a materialized thought of your Higher Self, modified by the acquired attitudes and habits of your conscious and subconscious minds. Because of this, the condition of your body its appearance and state of health can to a very large extent be altered by changing your habits, your self-image and your behavior.[4]" What we think about ourself, the world around us, other people and life itself drive us to create who we are. When illness exists, the physician must be sufficiently knowledgeable and skillful to help us to recognize and change those thoughts, behaviors and life patterns that are creating our illness. King continues, "Your body responds instantly on a cellular level to your every thought and feeling. Most often this takes the form of muscular or organic tension or release. By learning to master (i.e., direct) your thoughts and feelings, you can thus exert tremendous influence on your body. If you attempt to control or repress your thoughts and feelings, however, your body will rebel, instantly or eventually, with pain and/or dysfunction."[5]

The Huna concept of illness matches very well the work of researchers in the modern field of psychoneuroimmunobiology. We are our thoughts. Our thoughts either heal us and help us grow and evolve or they hinder us and/or hurt us. This hurt, pain and dysfunction are the illnesses we suffer. Clearly Huna works both for self healing and for facilitation of the skills and capacities of the physicians. It empowers us to positively affect our own life and body through how we live and think. It also demonstrates how illness and disease can take hold of us. By understanding Huna we can see that illness is an Intelligent act of the body in response to our thoughts, feelings, emotions and lifestyle. As we will soon see, illness is most commonly mediated through the stress mechanism. For our faulty beliefs and lies act against us not only on a cellular level but through the tension they create in the body, i.e., stress.

THE THREE SELVES

As we begin our discussion of the three selves, the lower self, the middle self and the Higher Self, it is essential that we once more remind the reader that the three selves, while discussed separately, are not separate from the individual. They are a construct of the Huna master that allows both discussion and a clear understanding of the interrelationships of the mind, body and spirit of the individual.

THE LOWER SELF

In Hawaiian, the lower self can be referred to in two different ways. As the *Ku* or as the *Unihipili*. According to King, Ku, the lower self, is a base or framework for something; a thing which can be changed or transformed, and something which can have emotional complexes. Psychologically, he says, Ku stands for what may be called the "body-mind," the organizing consciousness of the body, the receiver of information about the physical world (seen or unseen) and the executor of action.

Unihipili, according to Max Freedom Long, has three outward meanings, "spirit," "a grasshopper," and "leg and arm bones." This, he describes, is a long word made up of several short root words, each of which has several meanings of its own. It describes the subconscious so well that Long believed that anyone familiar with the modern terminology of the unconscious could clearly see that the kind of spirit it describes *must be* the subconscious. His description of the meaning of unihipili not only entertains the reader and demonstrate the mechanism of the hidden code of Huna but also tells us a great deal about the Huna construct of the subconscious.

In his book, *The Secret Science at Work,* Long describes the root word *u-nihi-pili* in the following way. "The roots describe it as a "spirit" that does things which the conscious-mind-self (orspirit) knows nothing about. It is secretive, and it works silently and carefully. It may refuse to do things it should do, and may be stopped by fear of punishment. (Root *nihi.)* It is a spirit which adheres closely to another spirit, in this case the conscious-mind-self, and it acts as a servant to it, accepts orders from it, but is often stubborn and refuses to obey. (Root *pili.)* It is a separate and independent spirit or self (root *u*) just as the conscious-mind-self and superconscious self are separate and independent spirits. This subconscious spirit is, usually, closely tied to the conscious-mind-self. It is a spirit which manufactures and handles vital force. It lives in the physical body and with this it covers itself as well as the conscious-mind-self, or *Uhane*, "the spirit which talks." It hides things (such as complexes). It is a spirit which is weakened if its supply of vital force is stolen from it by obsessing spirits."

The *lower self* is the oldest of the three selves and is also referred to as the low self, the unconscious self, the automatic or autonomic (after the autonomic nervous system) self. Anatomically it would incorporate the reptilian or hind-brain, the mid-brain, the spinal cord and the autonomic nervous system as its basic structure. It is called the lower self not because it is in any way less important or less developed but merely because its center is noted to be in the area of the solar plexus in the area of the mid gut. The lower self represents that part of us that is sometimes thought of as the unconscious self. The term, "unconscious," was first credited to Sigmund Freud in the late 19th century. However,when Freud first wrote about the unconscious the Hawaiians and other Polynesian nations had already been working with Huna and the lower self for more than two thousand years. When compared with the Huna concept of the unconscious, Freud's view was limited. He recognized only a few of the major characteristics of the Huna conceptualization of the lower self. Freud's understanding of the unconscious was limited by his particular definitions and construction of mental illness, psychosis and neurosis. He and his followers fell short in their description of the *unconscious* and its relationship to the physical body and the Huna concepts of the Higher, middle or lower selves.

To fully understand the lower self and what it is, one must look at its characteristics (See Figure-1).[6] In its most simplistic terms the lower self is the animal or instinctive self, the survival self. Within it lies the capacity to run the body automatically, maintain the involuntary functions and provide for growth and development of the physical attributes. The lower self interprets the genetic codes and the thoughts of man. It is, in essence, the genie within the bottle providing the capacity to maintain the body in what is sometimes a hostile environment. Just as the genie of Aladdin's lamp had to be awakened and commanded by a master, the genie within us also requires our command and direction to function. On its own, it is more than capable of managing the entire internal environment. But without its necessary connection to the middle and Higher selves, it is simply an eating and defecating machine. This is often seen in individuals who lapse into coma. The heart beats and food, if given, is digested. Yet something is missing. What is missing is the capacity to move, talk, react and respond to the external environment. There is no intelligent direction behind the physical mechanism.

While at first the physician may not be aware of it, he knows the lower

COMPARISON OF THE MIDDLE vs. LOWER SELF

MIDDLE SELF	LOWER SELF
Conscious self.	Sub-conscious self.
Human spirit.	Nature spirit.
Center is in the head.	Center in the solar plexus.
Subtle body is an astral body.	Subtle body is an etheric body.
Uses energy called mana-mana.	Uses energy called mana.
Has the power of will.	Has the power of wisdom.
Has thoughts and feelings.	Retains thought and emotional
Manifests itself through thought,	patterns. Manifests itself through
emotion and feeling.	the whole physical body as signs
	and symptoms.
Has short term memory.	Retains all memories
Rational and intuitional mind.	Literal mind.
Inductive and deductive reason.	Deductive thinking only.
Has free choice.	Ruled by lower self rules only.
Plays social roles.	Serves the social self.
Vocal, can speak in words.	Mute, can only speak in signs
	and symptoms.
The initiator.	The completer.
Decision maker	Carries out commands and orders.
Goal setter.	Goal achiever.
Teacher.	Student.
Master.	Servant.
Parent.	Child.
Programmer.	The programmed.

Table: 1.

self very well. He works with it every day. Yet not having studied it as a subject in school, he is often perplexed by it ratherthan using it to his advantage. The lower self, once understood and mastered, could provide the physician with a doorway into healing and understanding how to utilize the power of the lower self to get the results that he desires. If physicians would but open their minds to this ancient concept, they could see it as a tool that would allow them to understand the functioning of their patients. They could then understand how people create their own illness and how to assist them in becoming well again. Recognize your own lower self. See it as a friend and partner in your journey through life. Learn to work with it and how to master it. Make it your genie to bring you whatever you desire from your life. In the following chapters, we will guide you in discovering and maximizing the potential of your lower self.

THE MANY CHARACTERISTICS OF THE LOWER SELF

To best understand the lower self we like to think of it as a robot (or genie) that exists to maintain our inner well-being and provide us with what we need internally. Its goal is not only to ensure our survival but to help us to be successful and flourish. It maintains our life functions without need of our conscious awareness. It doesn't only keep our heart beating, digest our food, maintain our body temperature and process of excretion. It also maintains and controls a host of other physiologic and biologic functions such as our immune and repair systems which are necessary for us to maintain our ability to live and thrive. Built into the lower self is our survival mechanism, *the Fight or Flight system*. Later we will see how important this mechanism is to the creation of illness and disease. Without the lower self we would not be able to learn how to survive, for the lower self is in charge of *all* of our memory, our awareness of the past, present and projection of the future. To assist us in our survival, the lower self learns what works and doesn't work for us. It maintains this information in the form of *habits* which we form to protect us and pleasure us. The capacity of the lower self to form habits is crucial to our survival.

Habits, however, can be good and bad. While essential, they can also interfere with it our survival. Habits are learned programs of behavior and response. They allow us to respond automatically to situations without having to think them out, hence, without having to lose the time which might be essential to our survival. They also allow us to remember and perform complicated tasks and behaviors without having to think them through step by step. Think about driving a car and what an ordeal it would if you had to think through every step along the way. Driving a car is a habit, which requires that a series of decisions, muscular movements, actions and responses be used often without conscious thinking. Remember how hard it was when you learned to drive? You had to keep in mind all of thephysical and mental tasks steering, turning, watching in front of you, behind you, to your right and left sides, using the brake and the accelerator and doing it all in a coordinated and smooth manner. Consider what would happen if you had no way of storing the tasks you had learned. In such a situation you would have to relearn to drive each and every time you got behind the wheel. Think how difficult that would make your life. Consider how difficult walking or running would be if you had to relearn each step, as you did as a child, each and every time you wanted to run or walk anywhere. Our capacity to learn is mediated as a function of the lower self. It is essential to your well-being and ability to live your life as you do now. Without these learned programs, your life would be a living agony and, in fact, it is for many people.

The lower self might also be considered *the child within* (which we will discuss in greater detail in a later chapter). Like a child it is incapable of reasoning; it is literal about everything. In some situations, however, it can use a primitive form of deductive logic. This logic uses past experiences but cannot interpolate to the future. In this way, it is one-dimensional and egocentric. Everything you have ever heard, seen, thought and felt is recorded within the lower self. In order to protect you it uses this information constantly to check out every new and questionable experience. Since it cannot reason but it can deduce, it can make mistakes. It can confuse similar, yet entirely different situations because of their similarities. In doing so it often creates confusion and chaos within it. This is often one of the main reasons for anxiety and panic. When confronted with a situation that is in some way similar to a situation from the past, no matter how remotely, it reexperiences the past feelings and sensations, often misinterpreting it.

THE MIDDLE SELF

The second self is the *middle self* which is also referred to as the conscious mind, the aware self, the personality, or as the Hawaiians used to refer to it, the *Uhane, the spirit that talks*. The Uhane or middle self speaks, reasons, controls our voluntary actions, and uses intuition to know and experience the physical, material world that surrounds us. As Enid Hoffman describes it, it is the "self-in-charge."[7] The middle self is said to be located in the area around the heart. The primary role of the middle self is to relate the body to the world outside. It is the center through which we see, hear and feel the world around us. While the data from our sensory systems is processed through the lower self, it is only the middle self that can put this information together to form a picture of the world around us. For most of us, our waking, conscious self is almost as much of a mystery as the ever present but indefinable Higher or lower selves. Often when we think we know ourself the most, we do or say something that causes us to lose the sense that, our conscious aware self is meaningful. The middle self, while being that part of us that lives in the aware universe, relies heavily on the lower self for past memories and experiences to make sense out of the world. On its own, it could not survive for long for it would be unable to consistently recognize danger. It has no intuition nor memories of past experiences. It can think and reason very well but frequently its desires, wants, greed, aversions, fears, guilt and conflicts, which are all stored in the lower self, get in its way.

The main role of the middle self is divided into two components. The first is the most essential element, the mandate to survive. Once survival is accomplished, the second follows. Its role is finding food, building a society (for protection and companionship; the middle self often does not handle aloneness very well) and, ultimately, becoming a full-fledged human being. The lower self is, for all intents and purposes, an animal. The Higher Self, as we will soon see, comes as close as we can to being the God-like part of us. In the end, it is left to the middle self to tame the lower self, to connect with the Higher Self and to manifest itself as what we generally consider to be *a human being*. This process can happen early in life or late in life. In some cases,it doesn't happen at all.

There are three paths that the middle self must follow to make this happen. As stated above, its first path or task is to tame the lower self. This begins with first suppressing animal instincts, then learning to function in society (to walk, talk, have manners, ethics and logic); to become domesticated. And, finally, becoming educated either through schooling or through experiential knowledge. Our parents and society as a whole help a great deal with this aspect.

The next path is procreation. This occurs in two ways. The first way is *mating* and having children. The second way is through *creating a personal impact*, leaving a mark to prove that we were here. This is the root of our creativity and which we believe, is generated from the same force that urges us to have children.

The third path is also divided into two parts. The first is finding or creating our highest and best self and the second is defining our spiritual connection to the Universal Mother/Father, God, the Intelligence of the Universe. This is often thought of as *enlightenment*, the recognition of the existence of the Intelligence and, in its highest form, the ability to connect and become one with this Intelligence.

All three of these paths are part of the *Survival Mandate*. Each is a link to the integration of the three selves. Ultimately, when we reach full enlightenment we realize that the survival mandate is the essence of the Intelligence, the basis of the driving force that protects us until we reach the place where we recognize that we are, Sons and Daughters of the Intelligence of the Universe, and that we are immortal. While the personality (who we think we are) is a product of the middle self, who we really are, our essence, is the product of the integration of the three selves. When the middle self, thinking about itself and what it sees around him, comes to believe that it *is the real and only self*, conflict is generated. This delusion leads to an imbalance in which the middle self, thinking it is all alone, ignores the welfare of the lower self. The individual may also reject or disregard his spiritual nature and become caught up in the illusion of the material universe. When this happens the individual, really the middle self, feels alone, threatened and vulnerable. He needs *things* to make him feel better about himself. He looks for the love of others to justify his existence. He may judge himself not by his accomplishments or who he is but rather by what he can accumulate. Possessions may even become more important than life itself. This activates aconflict within him and he becomes ripe for illness and disease. If he is unable to manage this crisis in a healthy way he eventually becomes depressed or develops anxiety or other emotional illnesses. He is also a candidate for physical illnesses of all types.

Another important aspect of the middle self is its fragility. When some individuals face certain traumatic situations or experience a blow to the head, the middle self may lose contact with the lower self. In such situations memories of the past and plans for the future seem to disappear. When this happens the middle self, the conscious person, may suddenly feel that he has blanked out. He has no memories of the past, he doesn't know who he is and he can't remember people and situations that were once very close to him. Generally, in situations such as this the individual has an awareness of himself. He has sight, he hears, he feels and he experiences his body and its various needs. However, because he has lost contact with his lower self and his memory base, he may not know what to do with the information he is presently experiencing. In situations where this has happened the individual appears to have to start life over again. However, it is rare to see loss of ability to perform the common tasks of daily living, eating, using the telephone, driving, opening and closing doors, etc. These tasks just seem to be there as they have always been. While the injured person cannot remember who he is or where he comes from, he has no loss of these simple functions of daily living because these are programmed routines of the lower self and have little or nothing at all to do with the middle self. This demonstrates thatthe middle self has been injured and not the lower self. It shows that they are indeed two separate entities, each having separate roles and duties.

Table-1 illustrates the roles and differences of the middle and lower selves. It is essential to recognize that the middle self is the initiator, the decision maker, the chooser and the planner. It operates through the use of will power and issues commands to the lower self.

In order for the body to move, to turn or bend it must have a command from the middle self. This command may occur on the conscious level, that is, you say to yourself, "Open the door, I want to go out of the room." Or it can occur through commands given without conscious awareness, such as once again driving a car or riding a bicycle. It is the middle self that activates the right or left hemispheres of the brain but it is the lower self which interprets what the middle self wants. They must work together because if they don't, life becomes impossible. This is extremely important and will be demonstrated in a later section when we explain how blocks, complexes and faulty belief systems affect this relationship and become the basis of illness.

CONFLICT AND THE MIDDLE SELF

Since the middle self is the originator of thought, it is frequently the source of conflict. While the lower self's main role is physical survival, the middle self's main role is managing social survival. We suggested earlier that one of the major tasks of the middle self is to mediate creativity and toattain our highest and best self, our success. There are two factors that generate conflicts around these two functions. The first, is our *need for love* and second is our *need for power*.

The need for love is a primal need existing deep within us on an instinctual level. When we are able to experience being loved we feel good about ourself and we create a sense of *self-love*. However, when we do not experience a sense of satisfaction about being loved we can create a whole host of conflicts. Not loving ourself is the primary conflict which leads to illness and disease.

The second factor is *power*. This can often be seen as *will power* our ability to control ourself, and our recognition and leadership within the community. Based on our need to survive within the society we either feel accepted, loved and acknowledge or we feel frustrated and threatened. When our natural feelings regarding survival in our society are thwarted either by ourself or others we become jeopardized. Feelings may have to be repressed and truncated. Hence, emotions of fear and frustration are triggered. Love is diminished and anger, hatred and violence are stimulated. It is clear that as humans we are unable to love ourself and hate others. It is also clear that we are generally unable to hate ourself and feel successful. Because of these conflicts, the harmony andbalance between the three selves and the inner self is disturbed. Self-love is essential for well-being. Without self-love one cannot organize and utilize the middle self or the lower self to their fullest potential. When self-love is in conflict the immune system is thrown out of balance and once again the likelihood of illness and disease is increased.

The middle self affects the lower self through command and suggestion. The lower self, essentially being the servant, accepts every thought of the middle self as a direct command. What we say and suggest to ourself and others is not only listened to but taken as instructions and sanctioned as. Therefore, negative thoughts are negative suggestions and direct the lower self in a negative way. A simple thought like, "I hate it when I do that!" May trigger negative results in the form of aversions, loss of confidence and reduced capacity. Repeated thoughts of, "I hate myself," or "I hate it when I do that," may lead to feelings of worthlessness and failure of performance. Even worse, "I hate my life," "I wish I were dead" could eventually lead to the creation of a cancer or other chronic disease or illness that can take your life prematurely. People say these kinds of things very frequently. When we have told people about the power of the lower self in creating illness, it is not unusual for them to feel that we are exaggerating. Often they will tell us that they have said these things many times in the past and they are "still OK."Delusion number one: they are generally not OK for they usually have one or more medical problems, conflicts in their life and frequently are, to some degree, unhappy with their life. Delusion number two: it may take many years for them to experience the ultimate power of this type of conflict. One man, who argued with us at a lecture that the mind had little to do with the outcome of the body, was a smoker, an alcoholic and chronically unemployed. He believed that his inability to "get the right job was just bad luck." When speaking to yourself, always be aware of what you are saying. Speak absolutely and precisely. It is a good idea to think out what you are going to say and make sure that you are asking for, or suggesting exactly what you want to happen. Later on we will discuss this in greater detail when we introduce the Huna Prayer. At that time we will once again point out that our lower self is always listening and desiring to serve and create. An old adage says it best, "Be careful of what you ask for because you are likely to get it."

The happiest and safest way of living is to require yourself to love your lower self. Treat it with the utmost respect and caring. Admire it, see it as a partner, approve of it and accept it unconditionally. As Enid Hoffman says In her book *Huna, A Beginner's Guide*, "You are the most important self in the world to your low(er)[8] self, and your approval and love mean more thananyone else's. With your unconditional love it will respond and mature, enabling you to become co-workers." This statement is highly significant because just about every one of us wants this kind of love and acceptance from our parents. People, throughout the world, are daily telling therapists, "If my parents only loved me, accepted me and approved of me, I might be able to be an entirely different person." They imply they would not have the troubles they do today. If we were not able to get this kind of love, acceptance and approval from our parents then *we must give it to ourself.* We must become our own healthy parent, positively directing the lower self and loving both the middle and lower self in a non-judgmental, totally accepting way.

Physicians who are unaware of the relationship of the middle and lower self cannot truly help their patients get well. Perhaps because these concepts are not taught to physicians as part of their medical training, they are not personally aware of them nor are they able to help their patients get well through true prevention. It is also possible that it explains why there is such a heavy emphasis on treating with drugs and surgery; they have no other means with which to "fix" alower self that is in conflict and out of balance.

THE HIGHER SELF

The Higher Self is also sometimes called the High Self, the spirit or God-Self. In Hawaiian, it is known as the *Aumakua*. Long[9] refers to it as *the Utterly Trustworthy Parental Spirit* or occasionally as *the Totally Trustworthy and Benevolent Parental Spirit*. The Higher Self is connected to the higher spiritual levels of man. In is the part of us that performs healing. It can, when called upon in the right manner, produce instant healing. According to Long the *Aumakua* is made up of two primary roots. "*Au* which means 'older,' and completely grown or evolved so that it is superior in strength and wisdom and in trustworthiness. *Au* also means 'cord,' in this case the aka cord which connects it with its pair of lower selves." He continues, "*Au*, the root word, also means 'an action of the mind,' and 'a flow or current, as in the sea,' which symbolizes in the root the fact the High(er) Self performs an action with its mind in answer to our prayers to bring about *fulfillment* but at the same time there must be a mana flow to it. (A flow or current of water is a symbol for mana.)"

"*Makua*", he says, means, 'parent' or 'father,' and the root *ma* means 'to accompany,' pointing to the fact that it accompanies the low and middle selves through life as their guide. The same root has the meaning of 'to solidify' and this takes us to one of the most interesting beliefs found in Huna. It is the belief that all of the events and circumstances which we ask in prayer that the High(er) Self will cause to come to pass, are first formed in the aka substance as an invisible mold of the events, by the High(er) Self it having the knowledge and the power (if given daily supply of mana by the lower man) and that, 'solidified' or 'materialized' into the aka molds is the physical substance. When the 'solidification' is complete, the requested event or circumstance of healed condition suddenly appears as a fact on the physical level.

Once again through an example by Max Freedom Long, we get to see the power and use of Huna. The individual root meanings provide both ordinary and *non-ordinary* meanings which produce a word picture of the way Huna is used and the basis of the Huna belief. They also show how we can use Huna to heal ourself and get what we want out of life.

Another important element of Huna is the *Poe Aumakua*, or the "Great Company of Aumakuas." For the Hawaiians, the Poe Aumakua were essentially the "Utterly Trustworthy Family of Parental Spirits." In a sense they were guardian angels. If the Aumakua was not able to bring about the result asked for, he took the prayer on to still higher beings, the Poe Aumakua. Long also stated that Aumakua also means, "the god who is father." However he suggested that, "It was not an ordinary father." Through understanding the concepts of the Aumakua and the Poe Aumakua it may be considerably easier to see why the native Hawaiians could so quickly be assimilated into the dogma of Christianity. When the missionaries told them that they represent Jesus and his Father, the Hawaiians could immediately relate to Jesus as the Aumakua and the Father God and His Heavenly Host as the Poe Aumakua. To more clearly define this concept and the relationship of the Aumakua and Poe Aumakua to healing and its powerful spiritual connections, we would like to quote another section by Long from his book, *The Secret Science At Work.* You can see the power of Huna as well as the power of prayer. It shows us how the secret languages of Huna, as well as the secret language of the Bible, provide us with a source of knowledge, a science explaining how to heal ourself. It also establishes the support which "proves" that these prayers and beliefs work.

In the Judeo-Christian religions, God is referred to as *Jehovah*, if we were to translate the name of God into the secret language of Huna we will see that it holds several secrets. This translation might also help us to learn a lot about the concept of God and of praying to God. For many people, the concept of God seems quite enigmatic. Generally, when we want to believe in God we must accept His existence on faith alone. There is frequently a tendency to humanize God by thinking of Him as an old man with white beard; a deity with bolts of lightning in his hands. Whilesome people may think of this image as unreal, others have difficulty creating any picture at all. For those who understand the hidden language of the Bible or, in this case, Huna the picture takes on a meaning, one that can indeed be extremely real.

Max Freedom Long provides the following translation: "Jehovah" means "One who comes." When we translate this into Hawaiian it is, *kokoke*, which has the outer meaning[10] of "one who comes." Here is Long's translation of kokoke[11].

Ko: "To accomplish, bring about, fulfill (as answering prayer).

"To fulfill as an agreement" (or covenant).

"To obtain what is sought after."

"To put a law into force."

"To conquer or overpower" (have great strength).

Koko: "To replace a bone" (as in instant healing), "to set a bone."

"Blood" (symbol in Huna of the life of the body).

"To fulfill." (More emphatic word than just *ko*. The High(er) Self brings things to pass to fulfill promise to answer prayer.)

Koke: "To be near, not far, to come near to one."

"To be on friendly terms with one."

"To be attached to one."

"To favor one."

"To do instantly, quickly, immediately" (with the causative *hoo*).

Long continues, "There has been some groping about modern Christian churches of the less orthodox type for a concept of "God within" or "indwelling God" or "Father Who is within you." The idea has stemmed from certain New Testament phrases, perhaps especially from Jesus' words: "The kingdom of heaven is within you." We look into the Hawaiian language for words meaning "a god who dwells with or within one" and find *akua noho*, another of the several titles for the High(er) Self. The inner meanings are supplied by the root words as follows:

An *akua* was an entity or being superior to the middle self in intelligence or power or other attributes. It was superior in its ability to judge, and counsel and guide and protect. *Noho* means"to dwell with one" or "abide with one" as the High(er) Self coming on call to abide with the lower self and the middle self. But, while it is with the lower pair of selves, or in contact with them through the aka cord connection, all three selves are in a special condition or state of being, which is indicated by the second meaning of *noho*. This second meaning is a very important one: it is, "to have equal privileges with the low and middle self. This points to the fact that it must have its share of the mana or vital force of the man to enable it to function on the dense physical plane, and also to do its creative work of shaping the future on the invisible level of its being." Long further defines the Higher Self in the next section where he states, "Isaiah accurately sets down the Huna ideas of the High(er) Self in describing it as `Wonderful, Counsellor.' It is all this and more owing to its more evolved level of intelligence and higher knowledge. It is guide as well as guardian, if we will but open our lower selves and allow it to play its natural part in our lives on this level." "Isaiah," Long says, "also calls the High(er) Self the `Everlasting Father,' and that brings us right back to the father concept in the word for High(er) Self, Aumakua. Centuries after Isaiah's time, Jesus stressed the `loving father' aspect of God to the complete exclusion of the jealous and wrathful God of his forebears. This was no oversight on the part of Jesus. As we have said, he must have been an initiate of the ancient Huna teachings. As such he was able to become actively united with, or `one with the Father' at will, and so able to enjoy the aid of the High(er) Self inliving the life of the three-self man." "Jesus," he says, "called himself Son of Man, usually, but sometimes Son of God. When challenged for the latter, he quoted the ancient scriptures, `I said Ye are gods.' He was speaking, as did the Psalmist he was quoting, from his High(er) Self level."

The points we want to make are that, one, the Higher Self is part of man; two, it connects him to Higher Intelligence and powers far beyond his lower self level; three, by learning how to communicate with and pray to the Higher Self one can create or bring to himself *anything* he wants, including good health and well being.

We don't believe that we could have done a better job of describing and providing an understanding of the Higher Self than the words of Max Freedom Long. Long, however, had a good deal of difficulty in trying to describe what Huna is. He seemed to waver between calling it a *religio-philosophy* and *magic*. For us the decision is considerably easier. Huna is a system for preventing illness and healing illness. We believe the Bible to be a textbook of mental health. If you were to follow all of the principles and precepts presented in the Bible it is unlikely that you would get sick. Huna has only one principle, *creating no intentional harm to another*.

Huna is not a religion. Religion is usually defined as a system of beliefs and rituals centered around a belief in a supernatural being or beings, adherence to such a system, and a belief upheld or pursued with zeal and devotion. None of these exist with Huna. As stated previously, there is no dogma, no laws (except creating no harm to another) and no supernatural being. It is rather a description of how we work as human beings. As you can see from Long's words, the Higher Self is no more important than the lower self and the middle self, so there are no supernatural beings. Finally, no one asks anyone to pray or be devoted. The information on prayer simply explains how prayer works and how to utilize it more fully.

How does the Higher Self relate to the practice of medicine? The physician might say that the role of the Higher Self belongs under the auspices of the clergy. Physicians generally tend to ignore the spiritual side of their patients. This, we believe, is because they do not understand how the Higher Self works. Through Huna the physician has the opportunity to use his Higher Self to heal his patients as well as to help his patients use their own Higher Self to heal themselves.

CHAPTER THREE

Integration of The Three Selves

Huna suggests that wellness is best attained when the three selves are fully integrated into each other and are acting as a single unit. Illness, on the other hand, is more likely to occur when these three selves are out of harmony and balance with each other and therefore with the total person. While we discuss the three selves as if they are separate entities, as we have stated earlier, they are not at all disconnected. They are simply aspects of each of us. They are inseparable from us. However, how we organize ourself and what aspect we pay the most attention to can affect the balance of our own body/mind/spirit system. It is this balance we refer to when we discuss the need to integrate the three selves. In our society most people give a great deal more attention and therefore energy, time and consideration to the middle self aspect. Often the lower self is ignored, lied to, even neglected. While many people believe that going to church supports their spiritual nature, it does not. People often go to churchfor many reasons beyond their spiritual nature. These reasons include social contact, hopes of being on God's good side, fear or retribution, to please another family member, habit, entertainment, opportunity to confess, etc. While these may be reasonable reasons to go to church, they are hardly meeting the needs of the Higher Self. The Higher Self does not need an organized religion. That is why Huna is not a religion. Instead it needs recognition of its existence and utilization of its connection with the lower self.

We do not suggest that one should not be involved in an organized religion. That is an individual choice and is not discouraged. One can use Huna while belonging to any organized religion. Earlier we suggested that Jesus must have been indoctrinated in Huna for he speaks like a Huna master. We told you that the Hawaiians were easily assimilated into Christianity because they saw the principles of Huna and Christianity as being the same. We do, however, suggest that by understanding Huna and the power of the combination of the three selves, mind, body and spirit, you will see that the underlying principles of all religions are to create a personal connection with the Intelligence of the Universe, God, or whatever name you choose to give it.

THE LOWER SELF AND ILLNESS

The lower self controls the immune and healing systems. It is intimately related to our survival system and it is strongly affected by our thoughts and beliefs. In the following section we will look at how the lower self is so integrally related to our wellness and illnesses. As caretaker of our body, one of its major roles is to notify us of conflicts that can in any way diminish or impair our ability to survive. Illness and disease can generally be traced to conflicts and faulty beliefs which the lower self considers a threat to our survival.

Of the three selves, the lower self is the one which is most important to the medical practitioner and the individual who is sick. Primary healing is mediated through the lower self. Its major importance, however, is its association with the production of symptoms, emotional problems and illness. As the lower self is the manager of the physical body, emotions, memories and thoughts, it is most involved with the illness process. Its role is to control the physical body, manage the immune system, the body's healing and repair systems and the stress system. When the lower self is conflicted, it is likely that there is also conflict within the physical body.

The middle self is more often the creator of illness because of its propensity to create conflict and to get us into trouble. It is often unwilling to listen to the lower self in the early stages of illnesswhen the lower self tries to communicate that there is a problem. The lower self, when acting as the guardian of the body/mind, is quick to recognize an imbalance of any kind in the mind/body. Operating through an Intelligent mandate to protect, it attempts to communicate the imbalance to the middle self. What we usually think of as *the signs and symptoms of illness* are these Intelligent communications. These signs and symptoms generally begin as soon as the lower self has recognized that a conflict exists. In the earliest stages they are generally non-specific in nature, the symptoms of *stress*. If we listen to the lower self and correct the conflict the process is terminated and there is no more problem. If we are unwilling or unable to recognize the conflict the lower self will increase its urgency and the symptoms become more prominent and persistent. If the conflict is not corrected then, the physical body eventually begins to malfunction and the illness process takes hold.

The lower self is not always able to differentiate between external events occurring in our immediate surroundings, its memories of the past and our present thoughts. It is extremely important to understand that the lower self often confuses events, thoughts and memories. The lower self wants to give all of these inputs equal status and therefore registers them all as facts of life. It then organizes these inputs into an extremely complicated network of beliefs, facts,relationships and responses. It uses this network to correlate and classify every experience it is exposed to. We refer to this network in three different ways depending upon how it is used. First, it is the *Survival Center*. Within this survival center every input is checked to determine whether it contains information about some potential threat. In this way the lower self protects us from threatening events or situations presently unfolding. Secondly, it is our *memory data base*. This is the resource information pool from which our memories are taken and fed to our middle self to be considered. In both the awake state and the dream state this occurs. In the awake state it works somewhat like this: if we need to remember something like someone's telephone number, a date in history or a combination to a lock, we ask our self (actually the middle self asks the lower self). Once we ask the question, the lower self accesses our data banks, looks for and finds the answer to the question and then sends it up to the middle self. This system acts very much like a computer. You type in the question, the computer searches its data base and sends the answer to the screen. The third use encompasses our vast pool of unconsciousness memory; everything we have ever heard, seen, thought and felt, all external and internal inputs in our life. This aspect of the lower self provides us with the ability to recognize conflicts and implement potential solutions withouthaving to contact the middle self. Like the other two uses, it enables us to use this information to help us painlessly and often effortlessly to solve certain problems in our life. This represents the *problem solving capacity* of the lower self. Because of our inability to always tell the difference between thought and fact, we are not always able to resolve conflicts. In fact, we may create new conflicts for ourself. Without our knowing about this pool of knowledge, why it exists and how conflicts can reside within it, we are often unable to use it effectively. On occasion, conflicts cannot be resolved and the middle self is unwilling to listen to the warning signs and symptoms of the lower self. Try as hard as it will, the middle self is unable or unwilling to act and solve the problem. Eventually, as we stated earlier, illness erupts and these signs and symptoms ultimately surface. The stress reflex is tripped and *Stress Related Disorders (SRD's)* are triggered. We will discuss SRD's in greater detail in a later section.

While the middle self lives in a world of right and wrong, the lower self only knows what it is told. It can't decide right or wrong for itself. For the lower self, whatever you tell it is right, *is* right. Whatever you tell it is wrong, *is* wrong. However, it has no sense of what these really mean so it simply records within its complex memory network the labels as given to it by the middle self. As the lower self learns from the *feelings* we associate with right and wrong it simply parrots them back to us with an associated memory. If you believe that it is humiliating to show some part of your anatomy in public, it is the lower self that creates within you the feeling of humiliation. The humiliation you feel, usually referred to as an *emotion*, is actually only a memory. We will also refer to this memory as a *belief*. When two or more memories, habits, emotions, facts, data or responses are linked together we call this *a system of beliefs* or *a belief system*. While the individual *believes* that he is humiliated, this belief is no more meaningful than if he felt "wonderful" about the same situation. This is because either way, both are simply belief systems. The reason we experience different reactions in situations such as this is that we have given these beliefs different emotional response patterns and different powers to affect us. All beliefs are simply memories. But when we attach them to another type of memory, one of a particular emotion, they can be dramatically amplified. This emotion is like an electrical charge, positive for good feelings and negative for bad feelings. When memories become bound together, sometimes inappropriately, the charged feelings enters our memory network. Emotions have a very special attribute in that they affect the physical state of the body, causing a positive or negative physical response pattern.

THE ROLE OF THE MIDDLE SELF
IN ILLNESS AND HEALING

The middle self, being aware only of the conscious world, tends to experience a sense of detachment when it comes to illness. When we are sick we generally feel as if it is happening to us and that we have no control over it. While we know that it is occurring within our body we do not experience a connection to it except through our suffering, pain and the losses it causes. In medical practice it is extremely common for patients to comment that they have no idea why they are sick. They often see their illness as an imposition and sometimes even a test or a punishment. It is, therefore, not difficult to understand why the patient and the medical profession alike are so willing to blame bacteria, viruses and the environment for their illnesses. For one to *take responsibility* for his own illness he would have to at least consider the role he, himself, (that is the middle self) played in causing, creating or prolonging it. Since, as we have stated above, illness is generally mediated through the lower self, and the middle self usually has poor communications with its lower self, the middle self frequently feels no sense of responsibility. To appreciate the role of the middle self in creating or prolonging illness we must first look at how it functions. The middle self is the center of conscious awareness and is often confused with the personality. People generally believe that what they think is who they are. They don't want to think that they are responsible for being ill. To keep from worrying about getting ill, or being ill, or feeling guilty about causing their illness, the individual may *suppress* these thoughts. To do this the thoughts and ideas of illness and responsibility for illness are forced into the unconscious lower self. Unfortunately, the lower self doesn't want them either, so it may try to push them back up into consciousness. Whether it does this to make the middle self aware that these are important considerations or simply because the thoughts present a threat in some way to survival is not known. What we do know is that during the battle between the middle and lower self over these "undesired thoughts" the lower self is apt to see these thoughts as commands from the middle self.

Hence, "I don't want to be sick," can be interpreted as, "I want to be sick." The lower self believes that any thought or idea that comes from the middle self *must* be turned into reality. While this is true essentially of all thoughts and ideas generated by the middle self, we are only interested in those that relate to health and illness. We have discussed the concept of a person becoming humiliated by an experience and how their reaction is powered by emotions. As we stated, emotions are simply memories which, when linked together, become beliefs or belief systems.

What we have discussed in an earlier section has been related primarily to the way the lower self operates. But how does all of this relate to the middle self? First and foremost the middle self seesthis information differently. To the middle self, the sensations it experiences *are life*. The middle self doesn't consider what it feels as being "just a belief system" and especially not beliefs which have no definite meaning. To the conscious self these emotions all have real meanings, those that are fearful mean that something is threatening it. Those emotions that feel like shame either disgrace or embarrass it. The process begins when the middle self sends a thought picture to the lower self. For example, the conscious self finds itself in a situation which it interprets as compromising, this concept in the form of a picture is sent to the lower self for action. The lower self being under the control of the middle self, accepts that what is happening is fact. Since the middle self believes itself to be embarrassed this triggers feelings and emotions of embarrassment. If the belief is powerful enough these feelings cause a physical reaction (embarrassment or shame) which is immediately experienced by the middle self. Since the middle self takes responsibility for these emotions it sees them as part of the experience, caused by the events outside of it. It may or may not try to make sense of the total experience, however, since it must go through the lower self to retrieve its memories and the lower self is tied up with the emotions it may mix up its thoughts with the emotional charge and confuse the two. Hence, it believes that the event caused the emotional reaction and that the emotional reaction is entirely related to the specific set of events. It is unaware that its belief of the situation is the culprit not the event itself. This concept is likely to occur regardless of what the actual event is, or the specific cause of the emotion, or what the emotional charge meant in the beginning. The conscious self wants to believe what is happening to it. As the event unfolds and the emotional charge acts on the middle self, the middle self may look for justification, it vilifies the event and hence, the experience feeds itself. That is, we believe that our emotions are real and inherent in the event. For example, it is late at night, we are home alone, and suddenly we hear a noise just outside of our window. Our first thought might be something like, "Oh, my God there must be a burglar outside of the house." Immediately we experience a feeling of overwhelming fear, even terror, and with your heart beating rapidly and your palms soaking wet you grab your trusty baseball bat and you cautiously move toward the window. You spread apart the drapes and look out and there sitting on an overturned trash can is the neighbors cat. Within seconds you are laughing and the stress process begins to reverse itself. The powerful emotions of fear and terror, the stress reaction, were all created because of the belief that there might be a burglar outside of the house. However, this was never the case for the noise was created by the cat turning over the trash can. As we recognize that our emotions are simply recorded patterns of belief, belief systems, we can now recognize that we have the ability to *choose* how we want to feel in response to any specificexperience. Knowing this, we can learn how not to have our past memories and faulty belief systems choose for us.

One of the most common causes of illness and suffering are memories of past experiences which we have never been able to work through or experience fully. These memories are unknowingly stored in our lower self-data banks. They may continue to impact us throughout our life, as if they were real and happening in the now moment. Memories of the past can impact our present-moment decisions, control what we believe and act as a filter through which we interpret the world around us. They can manipulate our defense systems and determine how we act in life. Often the most problematic of these memories have existed since childhood and have absolutely nothing to do with the present. Past memories can be problematic, if we have been unable to *work through* these experiences and put them into proper perspective in relationship to our self and our world image. Whenever we are faced with an event from outside (as well as internally generated events, such as dreams or fears) we must process this information through our survival center that we will experience as being one of three responses. One, our survival is not perceived as being threatened. Two, our survival is perceived as being threatened. Or three, we are unsure whether or not our survival is threatened. If no threat is recognized then there is no special change. Life just goes on as it did before or is altered only by the actual events. If the survival center is unsure, it will either turn on the mechanism in some form of alert status or it will hold off until more evidence is brought to it.

If our survival is found to be threatened, however, the stress mechanism is immediately activated. This initiates the fight or flight process and all of the physiological, anatomical and psychological changes. This process lasts as long as the body/mind, usually the lower self, judges that there is reason to remain on emergency status. Once the system recognizes that our survival is no longer threatened, the mechanism is released and we go through a process of relief, release and relaxation.

What happens if this does not occur, if the threat is not considered over, or the lower self is confused about the reality of the threat? Then the body maintains itself in a full state of alert. It is as if it were at war awaiting an attack. While this process continues, it retains the full emotional, thought and memory pattern of this event suspended in a state of aggravated waiting. For all intents and purposes the attack is still in progress. When this happens, the conflict created is not fully experienced and worked through. Thebody/mind is left in the process of dealing with it. It essentially is waiting for either another attack or for resolution; and neither is happening. As days, weeks and years pass it remains current and on-going. The mind/body may suppress it in order to live its day-to-day life but it cannot release it. It sits just below the surface of consciousness as though in a state of siege. Only when the conflict is finally released and the mind/body accepts that the threat is over can the conflict be released. Once it is released, the mind/body can downgrade the level of awareness regarding this conflict from an alert status to that of a simple memory of past events. If the conflict remains unreleased, it can be reactivated at almost any time in the future. The full recall of the experience can leap into consciousness instantly and act as if it were happening right at that exact moment. This can happen no matter how much time has passed from the original event to when it is once again triggered. This can happen even though the individual is not aware that the conflict still exists. When activated, it can have the same charge it did when it occurred or even be more exaggerated than the original experience.

For example, a child has had the experience of watching his parent leaving the house to go to work. At that moment he feels totally abandoned and unloved. As he sees his parent fading intothe distance he cries and feels alone, helpless and vulnerable. This set of feelings may so threaten him that he feels a sense of impending doom. Since this conflict is not fully experienced by him, that is, logically perspective that the parent's journey is only temporary and that his parent will return in the evening, it remains incomplete as an ongoing threat (at least so he feels) to his survival. For years afterward, every time the parent starts to leave for work, this feeling of threat and abandonment returns. As he grows up he continues to have the same feeling when his partner or spouse leaves to go to work. He feels threatened and may frequently have a sensation of severe impending disaster or doom. Since he has completely forgotten the inciting childhood experience, we usually refer to it as a *complex*. Because he has never had an opportunity to work this trauma through he continues to be under the effect of this experience. A complex like this can last for many years, even an entire lifetime. It can only be terminated by the process of working it through. This could be done by talking to his parent about it and become aware that the parent would soon return. He could then relieve the fear thereby allowing the release of the associated emotions. Without this, it can only be eliminated by replacing it with either another more complex conflict or a new and healthier set of beliefs. Unfortunately, even though old complexes can be replaced by newer, healthier belief systems, this rarely happens spontaneously. These complexes usually become part of the warning mechanism of the body's defense system. Since they are ongoing fears or threats (real or imagined), they act to defend us from future exposure to similar threats. In that sense the lower self uses these *thought complexes* in a positive way. If only the individual who is affected by it were to know this, it might be possible to release some of its negative content.

THE LOWER SELF AND OUR SELF-IMAGE

The lower self is also the repository of the self-image. In a complicated process the lower self joins with the middle self to create a picture of the outside world and how we appear within it. The way we see our self is our *self-image*. The way we see the world is our *world view*. If we were able to fully separate our self-image from the way we see the outside world, we could become independent and free. We are not our body nor the events that happen around us; we are beyond them.

If, on the other hand, we are not able to separate our self from the outside world we may not have a clear sense of self-identification. We may only be able to identify with our parents, our political party, our race or religion. Then anything that we do not identify with can become a threat to our personal identity. Hence, situations like bigotry, prejudice, sexual and economic intolerance occurs because of confusion between self-image and world-image. In these processes, it is not unusual for people to confuse the way they see the outside world with how they see themselves in it. Ideas that we consider to be a problem get confused by people associated with these ideas. "All communists are bad." "All minorities are bad." "All rich people are bad." "All ..... are bad." If we have a clear distinction between our self and the outside world we are less likely to feel frightened. We are able to see shades of gray. We can recognize differences between the feelings we have and the things that cause them. When we see the outside world as challenging, it is likely that we will see everything as a challenge. When we are able to master our own needs we will be more ready to meet and master the world outside of us.

If, on the other hand, we see the outside world as frightening, fearful and overwhelming we may feel threatened and powerless. When the individual feels separated from the outside world, it is not unusual for him to find it difficult to relate to "other" people or groups. He might feel unworthy when he compares himself to others whom he invests with more power.

For example:

> Jane R. at twenty-two found herself addicted to crack cocaine. She had been brought up in an upper-middle class home with a relatively strict moral code. From an early age she felt insecure and frightened most of the time. In theprocess of establishing her self-identity she began comparing herself to her friends. If one of them got a new dress, she felt she too had to have a new dress. If one had a boyfriend, then she also had to have a boy-

friend. She dressed, ate, talked and thought like her friends.

One of her girlfriends, Susan, always seemed to be getting into trouble. Jane's parents told her that they didn't want her to associate with this girl because, she was the "wrong" type. Jane felt extremely threatened by her parent's rejection of her friend. She felt as if they were rejecting her. She soon began to emotionally move away from her parents. She resented her parents for giving orders (as it made her feel more powerless than she already did). Soon she rebelled entirely against their requests not to see Susan. Eventually, Jane's parents gave her an ultimatum, "Either you stop being friends with Susan or you move out of the house."

Since Jane's self-value was oriented around her need for her friends, the thought of giving up Susan was like asking her to cut off her right leg. She felt that she couldn't do it. She moved out of her home and she, Susan and another girlfriend, Marsha, took a small apartment together. Jane found it extremely difficult to say no to anything that Susan and Martha wanted. When Susan started using cocaine, Jane knew it was wrong but still could not refuse to do it when Susan and Marsha did. Within a short time she was addicted. To pay for her habit, Jane ultimately turned to shoplifting. One day she was caught and arrested.

Jane's story is just one of many situations that occur when there is difficulty creating a healthy self-image. It is not unusual for people like Jane to be led by others into doing things that create problems in their life. It is the feeding of faulty beliefs into the lower self that makes it unable to have a clear, distinct and healthy picture of who it and the middle self are.

The process of forming a self-image begins prior to birth with the creation of the lower self. It is generated by the multitude of information fed into it. With each thought, word or belief sent to it by the middle self, the lower self forms a picture of the outer world and its position in it. This process establishes a series of likes and dislikes, fears and guilts. Through this process, thought complexes are generated. Memories of the past and projections of the future are established. All of this is part of the formation of a code of morality, of beliefs and belief systems, about the self and the world it lives in. Ultimately from this process comes a picture of who we are and what the world is all about. Originally designed to support us in our survival, this picture can either work for us or work against us. While it often seems that who we are is created by what happens to us and the actions of others, this is only an illusion. Whether what happens to us is terrible or wonderful, it is ultimately the decisions we make about what happened that create (or determine) who we are and how we see the world around us. The decisions our middle self makes are sent to the lower self as fact and edict. Since the lower self cannot tell the difference between fact or fiction, truth or lie, it accepts whatever the middle self believes as fact and law. In the end, what we believe makes up the substance of our life. If these beliefs are accurate, we have a correspondingly accurate view of ourself and the world around us. If they are not accurate, that is, if they are faulty, then our view of ourself and the world around us will also be faulty.

Our ability to maintain our health and well-being is a factor of the harmony and balance between a healthy lower self and a lower self which is overburdened by faulty belief systems and negative thoughts. If we have allowed guilt and other destructive thought complexes to enter our lower self, it is likely that we will have conflict and illness at some point. If, on the other hand, we are able to locate and eliminate these unhealthy factors, we can strengthen and improve our chances for a long and healthy life for wellness and success.

In the next chapter we will look at how illness is caused and the relationship of the lower self and the middle self to causing it and the Higher Self for curing it. We will also see how our negative thoughts can impair our ability to survive as well as to diminish our chance for a joyful and healthy life.

CHAPTER FOUR

Huna and Medicine Working Together

The overall goal of this book is to dem onstrate that there is great value in forming a relationship between the practice of medicine and the study of Huna. The two are not mutually exclusive but rather are two parts of the same whole. Medicine is the technological aspect of healing and Huna represents the force that integrates the body with the mind and the spiritual aspect of the individual. Both aspects are necessary for complete healing.

The major problem we have seen is that medical doctors generally treat people without a full and complete understanding of the interplay of mind, body and spirit. They are not usually trained about the importance of how these aspects interplay to both cause and heal illness. When a patient is simply treated with medicines or surgery the physician loses the power and support of these crucial aspects of the individual. Ultimately, since they have agendas of theirown, not bringing their power into play can undo the work of the physician. When they are ignored, as they generally are, it is often common to see that the patient either does not get better at all or he improves but is not cured. Because of this, the process of medicine is generally directed toward the treatment of the individual. His patient's symptoms and problems are not cured but simply made better or relieved by medication. At first glance one might ask, "Isn't that what it is all about?" Here in lies the problem, for the answer is, No! When you watch carefully it becomes fairly easy to see that for most physicians covering up, masking, improving, or reducing symptoms is the main goal of their medical treatment program.

It is clear when one studies Huna that its main goal is cure; the complete elimination of the health problem with a total return to health and well-being. Another way of saying this is that the main goal of Huna is the complete and healthy integration of all parts of the Self. In Huna, the "Self" is divided into three parts and the concept of wellness involves a realization of harmony and union of these three parts. However, before we get into the description of the three selves and the Huna way of life, it is first important to compare and contrast the medical approach to illness with the Huna approach. This requires that we discuss a few salient points. The difference between healing and treating. How the medical profession measures success versus the way success is measured in Huna. And lastly, the overall concept of what the Western physician believes is the cause of disease and illness versus how Huna looks at this same issue.

THE MEDICAL PROCESS

The process of modern medicine is to diagnose illness and to treat it. This implies that the individual must get sick. Huna differs for it does not require the individual to get sick for it to work. In fact, Huna is ultimately about wellness. The Huna master is concerned with integration of the individual and especially the three aspects of the self which are so important to the health and well-being of the individual. He knows that illness comes from the division of the self and the inability of the individual to understand and repair this. The physician generally thinks about illness as if it enters into the body from the outside. It is brought in by bacteria, parasites, viruses and *germs*. He may believe that illness is caused by the individual's genetics. He believes that his patient has a predisposition to certain diseases and that diseases are unavoidable. He thinks about illness as *something that happens to us* rather then something that the individual creates himself. Most people believe that they are not responsible for creating their own illness(s). When an illness strikes them, they consider it to be an unfortunate thing which just happens to you due to a stupid reason such as being careless. The Huna master thinks of illness differently for he sees it as an intelligent act of the body, a response to specific thoughts or conflicts. To the Huna master illness is a *clue to the past*.

HOW IS ILLNESS CREATED?

For the most part the concept of illness is pretty much taken for granted in our society. Most people, not just the medical profession, think of illness as a negative state. They believe that it is caused by either organisms (bacteria, viruses or parasites) or environmental, chemical or other phenomena (injury, war or crime) that attacks us from outside of ourself. In the case of autoimmune diseases and genetic diseases, our own tissues attack us. In the former we have no specific idea why and in the latter we consider that our genes are responsible and there is little, if anything, that we can do about it other than accept it. Only in a few situations does either the medical profession or the general public believe that we ourself have some responsibility in the creation of our own illnesses. In short, most people believe that there is little or anything that we as individuals can do to protect ourself or to eliminate illnesses. While it may often appear that we are helpless and that only the medical profession can take care of us once we have become sick, nothing could be farther from the truth. This concept of illness coming from outside of us is, in fact, a relatively new concept with origins in the 16th century. It gained great momentum with the separation of religion from medicine and the discovery of microorganisms. Prior to the 16th century illness was looked at somewhat differently. Before organized medicine,in the days of superstition in the dark ages, illness was believed to be caused by something we did, thought or felt. While still tied to a belief that illness came from outside of us, the organized religious view was that it was related to decisions and choices we made and beliefs that we held. The more recent concept of germs was preceded by belief that we were invaded by evil spirits.

Huna had a slightly different view of illness. The Huna master considered that illness was a sign of one of two things: complexes or spirits. Complexes are faulty belief systems that interfere with the body's ability to function normally. When complexes exist, the body's ability to protect itself or heal itself is diminished. The concept of spirits, on the other hand, can be seen in two ways. One, as actual spirits of other beings or their aka bodies loosened by death or injury; or two, as thought complexes that have taken on a life of their own and take control of the individual.

In either case the aspect that we are interested in throughout this work is the relationship of illness to our thoughts, beliefs and the complexes and conflicts we create for ourself. What we will investigate and discuss is the notion that illness is created not by germs or evil spirits, nor by our tissues attacking us but as the consequence of an Intelligent system which we are generally unaware of and, hence, runs out of control.

INTEGRATION OF THE THREE SELVES

Illness is an intelligent act of the body letting us know that we have unresolved conflicts that we must solve in order to live life fully, competently and healthfully. This process is Intelligent because it suggests that recognizing and solving conflicts is not only important to our well-being but it is part of who and what we are. Our nature is to learn and grow and, if possible, to reach a state of enlightenment. Enlightenment requires that we solve problems so that we can control our own destiny. Without true enlightenment we can never be free and without freedom we are merely slaves, lower selves without connection to our Higher Selves. If we operate only in our middle selves, we are aware of the world around us but our body becomes an adversary, fighting and attacking us again and again. To live with our head in the heavens, in the Higher Self alone, however, leaves us living with our head above the clouds. From this position we can no longer see the road we travel on nor have any sense of our physical self. This further disconnects the three selves.

In the end, the Huna master believes that the only way to be fully alive, and to maintain health and overall well-being is to integrate the three selves. It is to this overall purpose that illness exists; tohelp us find and eliminate conflicts. As we shall demonstrate throughout this book, the role of illness is to assist us in finding complexes, fears and guilt that impair the relationship of the three selves and our connection to the Intelligence of the Universe.

WHAT WE BELIEVE CAN KILL OR ENLIGHTEN US

On a simplistic level *what we believe is who we are.* It colors our relationship with not only the world around us but with our own self. We are often so caught up in our own beliefs that we consider them to be truths. When we live by faulty beliefs we have considerable conflict in our life. Since we don't like conflict or pain we often either suppress our feelings or project them outside of ourselves. Hence, the other guy is the problem, the germs attacked us from the outside or I never saw it coming are the most common kinds of things we hear in the medical profession today. Few people stop and say, "I am fully responsible. My logic and facts were faulty, I drew the wrong conclusions and by acting on these conclusions I created a problem for myself." While this might at first sound ludicrous, it is not. Accepting responsibility allows us to take that most important next step which is learning from it. Blaming it on the other guy, a bacteria or fate keeps us from moving forward. In the end life is about the experiences we have and what we learn from them. While our society spends a great deal of time and effort on blame, retribution and guilt, it has littleenergy or time left over for learning, growing and evolving. The same is true for each of us individually. We must learn from our experiences in life and we must then grow from this knowledge.

Scientists are now finding that the immune system is directly affected by our thoughts. Positive thoughts trigger positive innervation and stimulation of the immune system while negative thoughts adversely affect it. Negative thoughts, fears, anger, rage, repressed feelings and emotions all draw energy away from the body. They reduce the capacity of the immune system to fight disease and to protect us. More accidents happen and we are more negatively affected by the forces of the environment. These negative processes stimulate the stress mechanism because they act as potential threats to our well-being, to the way we want our world to be. Ultimately if we do not learn from these processes we move into chronic stress and then Stress Related Diseases. Stress Related Diseases are often missed by the medical profession because the medical profession has no good, operating definition of stress.

Our definition: *Stress is the physical, chemical and biologic reaction to the difference between the way you want the world around us to be and the way it really is.*

STRESS

Stress is a major problem in the general public, industrial workers and professionals alike. Problems caused by stress are seen in medical practice possibly more often than any other problem. Stress itself is a normal part of life. Every living creature exhibits the stress response in one form or another. Its role is to protect us from the world around us, especially from anything that might threaten our life or well-being. Often referred to as the *Fight or Flight Response*, the Stress Mechanism not only helps us become aware of any potentially threatening situation, real or imagined, but also allows us to react by either fighting to protect ourself or running away from the danger. This mechanism bypasses thinking and decision making. This accelerated response time allows us to act faster than we might if we had to think the situation out, decide what to do, make plans and, finally, act. The system acts to bypass thought, therefore saving precious time in reacting. The stress mechanism is the basis of many illnesses and diseases that are usually not considered related to stress. While stress itself is a normal part of life, once it becomes persistent or recurrent, chronic stress becomes an abnormal process. If it is not reversed or eliminated, it can eventually lead to the breakdown of the body's chemical and organ systems as well as its ability to defend and heal itself. The net result is a series of signs and symptoms which first represent the stressmechanism itself but later progress to become signs and symptoms of the failure of the defensive systems and finally, into the realm of illness and disease, even chronic disease and death.

The process of these signs and symptoms can be divided into five groups, stress, dis-stress, dis-ease, disease and chronic disease. The earliest stages stress, dis-stress and dis-ease have relatively vague and non-specific symptoms and signs. They are commonly missed by the medical professional who is not trained to look for such vague and irregular manifestations. Once the symptoms and signs reach the level of disease or chronic disease, doctors generally will easily recognize the positive physical findings and relate them to specific disease patterns. In Figures: 3-1 & 3-2, we have demonstrated first the flow of levels of illness from wellness through stress into dis-stress, dis-ease, disease and chronic disease.

WELLNESS-STRESS-ILLNESS CYCLE

Wellness → Stress → Dis-Stress → Dis-Ease → Disease → Chronic Disease

Figure: 3-1.

As you will see in the next sections, stress is often created because of blocks, complexes, fears, guilt, anger, and rage. This occurs most often when these stresses and their associated emotions are suppressed, ignored and not acted on. When this happens the issues underlying the stressreaction becomes a threat to the self-image, the ideal-self, as known to the lower self, or the way the conscious self believes the world should be. The lower self, wanting to perform its job well, requires that the middle self make good healthy, accurate and loving decisions. When it doesn't, conflict occurs. This conflict is created by the difference between the way the conscious self wants the world to be as well as the way lower self needs the world to be and the way it really is. This becomes even more significant when we realize that we have usually created the world around us to be exactly the way it is. While the middle and lower selves do not necessarily have to *like* everything that happen to them, they must at least be willing to accept what is happening to maintain health. When one cannot accept his life he will in some way feel threatened. As the level of threat increases in conflict between what is and what is needed, stress is generally generated.

On the other hand, when the way we want the world to be and the way it actually is match, we will often find ourselves experiencing happiness and joy. This is a positive experience and in the end, one that heals us. It is for this reason that we suggest that the ultimate goal for healing is problem solving. Helping to match the desires of the middle and lower self by actively creating the world to be the way they want them to be or actively changing what is desired to the way the real world is. This is demonstrated in Figure: 3-3.

REVERSIBILITY OF THE
WELLNESS-STRESS-ILLNESS CYCLE
Life ↔ Stress ↔ Dis-Stress ↔ Disease ↔ Chronic Disease ↔ Death

Figure: 3-2.

In Figure: 3-2 we demonstrate several important principles. Each level of stress from distress through onset of chronic disease is for the most part completely reversible by resolving (usually through problem solving) both the original conflict and whatever secondary conflicts are created subordinate to them. If the original and secondary conflicts are not resolved by the onset of a chronic disease, the likelihood of resolution rapidly diminishes and may even entirely disappear. Once a disease process is started, any disease process, it takes on a life of its own and may no longer be reversible and may even lead to death. In the stage of chronic disease, anatomy, physiology and even psychology are so altered that even if the original conflict and secondary conflicts are resolved the process has generally progressed much too far to allow reversal and return to wellness.

RESOLVING ILLNESS
Disease → Dis-ease → Dis-Stress → Wellness

Figure: 3-3.

BLOCKS, COMPLEXES AND CONFLICTS

In the previous section we discussed a number of very important points about Huna which differ from what we consider to be standard medical practice. The role of the physician as a healer rather than a treater requires that he not ignore the needs of his patients **until** they get sick. He must look for and recognize signs of impending illness or indications that his patient is moving on a course toward illness. The major dilemma has been that the "modern" physician doesn't always see this as his role. The result is that he often sits by and literally watches his patient fall into illness so that he can rescue him and "play" doctor. Some physicians might answer this call by saying, "My patient doesn't come to me **until** he is sick." Another might add, "It is not my business to interfere in my patient's life nor tell him **how** to live his life." Yet another physician may say, "Everything you have said is nonsense and you should be ashamed of yourself; you're a charlatan." In the end, the question should be, "As a caring, loving physician how far and what must I do to get my patients well?" Is just working to get sick people well being a good physician? I believe that a **great physician** is one who not only helps people to keep from getting sick but also does everything he can to eliminate sickness. Huna provides a basis to see the world differently -- to see that illness can be prevented and eliminated.

The construction of the Huna prayer can be looked at as a system to solve problems and clarify life goals, to plan and to create a sense of structure and wellness which leads to the development of one's highest and better self. It is a problem solving technique, for when done well, it helps the individual to identify problems, consider solutions and think through and plan important parts of their life. In this sense it reduces stress, diminishes the likelihood of error, increases self-esteem and helps the individual to be more successful and, hence, less likely to have conflict and illness. One can look at this model for healthy living and then compare it to the enormous amount of stress related illnesses that presently exist and decide which is a better route. Is it better to reduce stress related illnesses or allow them to continue by simply treating them with medications and never solving any problems? Earlier we discussed the role of stress in producing Stress Related Disorders (SRD's). Huna adds to this model by allowing us to more clearly recognize the interaction of mind, body and spirit both in the creation of SRD's and in healing them. Through Huna we can see that the creation of belief systems (decisions, orders and commands) by the middle self can lead to conflicts and chaos. In the remainder of this section we look at the complexes, blocks and distortions that lead to stress and eventually to stress related disorders.

A fact that is often ignored and suppressed is that we live in a **sick** society. As the years go by it appears to be getting sicker and sicker. The reason is we are refusing to take responsibility for our actions and the actions of others. We are always making the other guy the bad guy. We are projecting the reason our life doesn't work onto someone else making it *their* fault. We are unwilling to admit when we are wrong and learn from it. We make being wrong a sin instead of an opportunity to learn and grow. We are hooked on images of the way it should be instead of creating what we really want out of life. The amount of unhappiness that exists around us is astronomical. The law serves the viewpoint of the few and makes criminals instead of solid citizens. The national pastime is making money, not increasing our personal self-value. We prize things above people. People are exploited for personal welfare and wealth.

In America we have no national goals. Throughout the world there is no pride in growth and self-evolution. There is no connection to the human species and the planet earth. It doesn't work and few, if any, leaders are willing to wrestle with solving the problems. When the individual lives life this way it is a prelude to disease for there is no harmony; only imbalance, chaos and discord. The immune system can't function well for long in these conditions. For our society it has meant war and pestilence in a land of plenty. For the individual, it means illness and affliction. Ultimately the only way to save the world is for each of us to recognize this and look inward to eliminate the elements of disorder within our own personal world. When we can make ourselves well and create our long term well-being, we generate the potential of wellness and well-being for the rest of the world. It has been said before, "The rest of your life begins with what you do today." No one can solve the problems of the world until his own problems are solved. What keeps us from solving our problems is our own self.

Huna describes thought forms which live within us and block or impede our ability to function healthfully and normally. These are often referred to as *complexes*. They are negative beliefs that interpose themselves between the requests and commands of the middle self and the action of the lower self. For simplicity's sake we call them *Belief Systems* or more specifically, *Faulty Belief Systems*. These belief systems sabotage us. They *limit* our abilities and potentials. They are *fears* and *conflicts, remembrances of negative experiences* and *old hurts*. They operate through the stress mechanism. They once had an intelligent reason for existing; to protect us. Often they start to develop with the development of the nervous system. They occur initially as inputs from our nervous system about real or imagined dangers, threats or potential threats. Rather than reading them simply as input of information, for some reason, we give them power to affect some or even all of our future responses to the events of our life. For the most part they act as a filter; they screen the information we receive for the rest of our life or until they are either eliminated or replaced. They can cause us to see the world differently from the way it really is. Since by definition they are negative (there are also positive ones but we will discuss these later in greater detail) they block out positive information and force us to see what they want us to see.

For example: bigotry is a block which forces us to only **be able** to see a preset belief system about people of certain religions, races, skin colors or ethnicity. Rather than seeing a person as an individual, the bigotry filter forces the view point that **all** people of a particular group are bad, or dumb, or stupid, or worthless, etc. The enlightened person knows that this viewpoint is not true but the bigoted person can see nothing else. While the person who is the victim of the bigotry certainly suffers the bigoted person suffers too, because he or she is living in a lie, unable to see and experience the real world. This limitationdistorts not only their world-view but their self-view. When the faulty belief system is bigotry, we usually don't feel too sorry for the individual and may instead see them "as the bad guy." However, knowing that their faulty belief system is based on low self-esteem, feeling like a failure, a fear of men or even a need for illness, then we may be able see them more as casualties of life. In the end all of these complexes, fears and restrictions are simply faulty belief systems which we have accepted at some time or other during our life. Like any other belief system they can be thrown away at any time. We see this happening all around us, every day of our life. Someone says that they hate a particular food until they try it and decide they like it. A women thinks a particular style is awful until she tries it on and finds she loves it. Faulty belief systems exist whenever we "hate" something or are afraid of something, feel threatened by something, etc. They exist because at some point in our life we believed that they in some way presented a threat to us. They triggered the stress mechanism and power was given to them as real or potential enemies. In this process we made a decision about them or created an opinion about them and we have continued to give this decision or opinion power. They continue to be powerful because we continue to allow them to take power. We may even reenforce their power over and over again. To do this we generally create or find *evidence* that *proves* that this belief system is right (continues to deserve power).

A good example of this is the story of Margret C.

> Margret had been molested by her father and her uncle a number of times when she was a child. She was told each time that if she told anyone they would deny it and she would be all alone. Margret was terrified that if she told anyone her father or uncle would hurt her so she kept the molestations a secret. As Margret grew up she found that she was unable to trust boys. Throughout high school she refused to date. She wanted to participate in school functions but the thought of being alone with a boy was much too scary to consider. In her second year of

college she met Jeff. He was very nice, didn't push her and was persistent in his desire to go out with her. After six months of asking he finally told her that he would soon have to stop if she "was unable to get past whatever block she had about going out." At first this infuriated her. She felt as if he was pushing her and his pushiness frightened her. However, she really liked Jeff. He was fun to be around, he seemed honest and he hadn't "put any moves on her." After thinking it over she decided that she really wanted to keep their friendship and that she would miss him if he stopped "being there." Something else happened about the same time. One of the girls in her dorm told everyone that she had been molested as a child. She later told Margret that she had joined a Rape Crises group and had been able to work through a lot of her anger. She told Margret how she had suffered for a long time and finally decided that she had to do something about it. After their discussion Margret was a changed woman. Without any other outside help she came to a sudden realization that her father and her uncle were the sick ones and she hadn't done anything to create what happened. Later she told me, "Why should I suffer from their disease? I made up my mind right then and there that I would live a healthy, normal life and that I was now old enough and smart enough to be fully responsible for my own sexuality." Margret called Jeff and asked him out. When I met Margret and she told me her story she and Jeff had already been happily married for six years. They had two children and another one on the way.

When I asked her how she had come to such a momentous decision she answered, "I just realized that I could no longer feel guilty for something I never had done. I was a child and they took advantage of me. For years I felt guilty that I must have done something to bring it on, that I somehow caused it to happen. I felt ashamed, I was constantly scared, I didn't think I would ever be able to trust another man. When Debra told me what had happened to her I suddenly realized that it was my father and my uncle who were sick and not me. Debra had felt the same way that I did and I realized that as a child I had no other way to feel. Now, as an adult, I could feel and believe anything I wanted. I was a good person and I deserved to have what every other woman has, a loving, caring relationship. The thought that I would allow what happened almost 15 years before ruin my opportunity to have a healthy relationship made me rethink my decisions and change the way I had been thinking."

I don't think that I have ever heard it put so eloquently or powerfully. "Rethink my decisions and change the way I had been thinking." Unfortunately, for every person who does this, there are many others who remain stuck in their old, useless, destructive and power draining decisions. Margret was lucky (and also ready) that she was able to recognize that her old childhood decisions and beliefs still controlled her even years after the events that created them had faded into mere memories. In a sense that is often what these lies and distortions are, just old memories. Painful, hurtful, demeaning, power draining old memories. They have often been dead and gone for years. Only the decisions and remembrance of them, like wormy old bones, still exist in the present. Yet they still affect us. They control our behavior, affect our present decisions, dominate our life andrestrict our living.

The Huna practitioner knows that these blocks, guilt feelings and fixations (fixed ideas about the way we think things are or were) exist and he knows that they can impair our ability to be who and what we want to be. He knows that they take joy out of life, that they cause illness, emotional instability, anxiety, panic, depression, fear and premature death. He also knows that these conflicts can be eliminated. He knows that they can be replaced by healthier and more helpful reality-based belief systems. The removal of these complexes and faulty belief systems are always part of his treatment program. He also knows that the ability and willingness to give them up must be decided upon by the individual himself. Unlike the western medical doctor who sees these complexes as impossible to eliminate, the Huna master sees them only as ideas that can be changed. He gives no power to them considering them as lessons that the individual needs to learn and not as insurmountable road blocks or inherent within the person's make-up. He knows that all one needs to do to eliminate them is to know that they are there; to stop fighting them, make friends and then to replace them with a belief that is healthier and better. The Huna master is a realist and knows that not everyone is ready to release his blocks so he instructs his patient to live with them and just know they are there until he is ready to do awaywith them. He then sets up a series of exercises which he refers to as *prayers*. Their purpose is to reprogram his patients, their blocks, fears and their future. The prayer is designed by the individual himself with the help of the Huna master to formulate a newer healthier set of belief systems, goals and decisions. The Huna master then teaches his student how to empower his prayer and remake his future.

HOW DO COMPLEXES COME ABOUT?

As we have already suggested, complexes are developed through life experiences (possibly even past life experiences). They are reactions to these experiences. While fun and good experiences are remembered they usually do not affect the individual negatively. When a negative experience occurs it generally trips the stress mechanism, hence it is registered as a threat. The degree of actual threat is often less important than the degree of perceived threat. On occasion a meaningless event can be perceived as meaningful and threatening and ultimately leaves a lasting scar. In this sense these experiences are scars on the psyche. Complexes trigger stress and impact overall memory. For example, an individual picks up a hot pot and gets burned. He remembers it all of his life but he doesn't necessarily have to react negatively. He can choose to check out all other pots on the stove to see if they are hot. If the event is *perceived* as threatening he may empower it with such negative emotions that whenever it is triggered it becomes as real as if it were happening at that exact moment. The degree of energy or power instilled into it may be related to the severity of the event. For example, a woman who has been raped may be so traumatized by it that she shuts down. The normal emotional response would be to realize that the event was criminal and severe but able to keep the perspective that it was one single event and that she survived it. A shutdown, however, causes a repression of the feelings, that is, an inability to deal with them. The situation and its emotional impact are essentially *locked* into the woman. She then has no way to deal with it, no way to release it and process it to bring it into reality. Hence, in the future, any threat that reminds her of the rape (and these situations can be very loose) can trigger the full emotional response of the original event. While in a normal situation we experience stressful situations, we also generally process them through reality factors, we discharge our emotion and release the emotional charge. In the situation described above this does not happen. Any situation that triggers it may allow for an instant replay and creation of energy without discharge.

Here is an example of the simplicity of a block and the problems it can cause. While working with a patient who was having menstrual cramps, we were able to determine that she had several complexed beliefs about menstruation. She felt as if menstruation was a condition which was out of her control, "How would you like to have blood come uncontrollably out of your penis each month?" She asked me. Secondly, there was conflict about the fact that she had decided earlier that she wanted no more children, "It seems so useless to have a menstrual period each month when I have already made the decision not to have any more children." Thirdly, "I can't always tell when my period is going to come so having a period is quite distracting and annoying." This combination of the inability to control her body, and of the uselessness and inconvenience of her periods seemed to make having menstrual periods a miserable event. This combination established the grounds for her menstrual periods to be painful. Since she was ready to do something about it, we discussed her creating a ritual to transform the situation. We suggested the following three steps.

The first step: To help her understand her lower self better we gave her an assignment which would bring out all of its conflicted images and faulty beliefs about menstruation. We asked her to write out a list of everything she believed about menstruation, menstrual periods, femininity, uteruses, reproduction and reproductive organs. Once this list was completed we looked at all of the responses. We crossed out all those that were faulty or negative and as we did this we wrote a new list of all of those things which were true and positive. When she completed the list of positives, the negative faulty belief list was burned in a small ceremony to let the lower self know that she no longer wanted it to operate from these conflicted beliefs and images.

The second step: Using the positive list, she wrote a blessing ritual which blessed and praised the lower self for maintaining her ability to reproduce even though she *chose* not to have any more children. Each positive was worked into the prayer either as a blessing or a direct statement. Next, she was to praise the lower self for the ritual of cleansing the uterus so that each month she could start anew, clean and healthy. She was then to show an appreciation for her femininity and the presence of her female organs. She was to praise their usefulness in preparing and allowing her to get pregnant, when she wanted to, and be able to have children if she wanted. She then created a prayer for her female hormones and their role in her femininity, procreation, protecting her against heart disease, premature aging and for the role they played in her sexuality. In order to deal with the "inconvenience of not knowing when her period would start" she asked for a small but noticeable degree of cramping to let her know that her period was about to start. The image she used was that of a soft door bell which lets you know when friends have arrived.

The third step: It is important to perform this ritual and ceremony each month upon the onset of the menstrual period for the next several months. The ritual is to welcome it with joy and pleasure as one welcomes an old and valued friend. This ceremony lets the lower self know that you appreciate its work in providing menstruation and that you especially appreciate the fact that it is not painful nor excessive and that it is a normal healthy biologic function. In this woman's family, just about every female had a hysterectomy in her forties. She did not wantto have a hysterectomy. It was her sense that the menstrual cramps had some relationship to the family history, yet she had no specific connection. The Huna prayer and ritual was created to help her avoid a hysterectomy as well as the menstrual cramps. The end result was that her uterus was no longer her enemy but rather a friend in a partnership of femininity.

Another interesting story is that of June R.:

> June R. was 42 years old, having severe PMS and virtually out of control in her life. She was unable to work, in desperate debt, having relationship problems and tortured by a history of childhood molestation by her father. Her diet was generally OK but it was much higher in calcium than magnesium and because of her frustration she ate a fair amount of sweets, especially chocolate, and often used alcohol to bury her pain. Because she was unable to work, she saw herself as a failure. "Two years ago I had a wonderful job; I loved it. I got a wonderful sense of satisfaction from it. I felt good about myself. Then the PMS symptoms began being a problem. Sometimes I would get so depressed I would feel suicidal. Lately, in the week before my period I am suicidal all day long. It has gotten to the point that I must drink to dull the pain. In this situation, a poor diet triggered the premenstrual syndrome and with it many of the "nightmares" that had not been dealt with in the past were let loose. With June's inability to do herjob, her self esteem was also lost. While the simplest form of treatment would be to bring her PMS symptoms under control, this would not be enough for June on its own. In order for June to return to wellness she would have to deal with her alcoholism, the experiences buried in her molestation, her feelings of insecurity and as important as anything else, her debt. To do this we first placed June on a rigid anti-PMS diet. However, because of the severity of her symptoms she requested a short-term course of Prozac to help her get control of her life. Trading one addiction for another was not our goal so we made an agreement to set up a Huna prayer system, much like we described above, wherein she would begin to write down a list of all of the positive and negative images and beliefs she had about herself. We then picked out her past negative experiences and the negative images they caused. Next we listed all of her positive qualities. Since she had made the list of positive

and negative images and qualities, all of the positive reflections were her own and hence the lower self would be more likely to believe in them. A small but powerful ritual was then created wherein she read aloud each of the negative images, tore them from the page and then burned them in a ritual fire. Finally, we created a positive prayer to replace all of the old negative images with a new and brighter more positive view of herself and outlook for the future. June would say this prayer daily until she felt good about herself.

The Huna master also recognized that old faulty beliefs do not die easily. In the course of working with people who suffer from Stress Related Disorders, we recognized that these faulty belief systems acted as if they have a life of their own and it is often separate from the rest of the individual's life. Attempts by psychologists, therapists and analysts to remove them often caused such great pain and discomfort that as a result, the individual left therapy. Hence many therapists also believe that you can't change people. The faulty logic here is that the individual himself generally *wanted to change*, he just didn't know how and, unfortunately, often the therapist didn't either. This suggested that some hidden power was at work. It might have been easy to fall victim to the old philosophy that people just can't change but we recognized something different and this led us in a new direction. These old faulty beliefs remained attached to their lower self. That is, a faulty (but often necessary) decision made by a three year old simply didn't disappear when the individual turned four or five or six or even ten or twenty years old. It persisted as part of the individual's memory base. In doing so it became, as the Huna practitioner calls it, a complexed belief or thought, a block or a fear. We refer to this process as the *Child Within,* a symbolic representation of that part of the person that didn't die but still exists under the many layers that have been covered over by growth and age. In actuality, the *Child Within* is simply a set of beliefs, usually faulty, that persist as part of his personality. Generally, he is unaware of its existence. He may from time to time wonder why he acts the way he does, but just like most of us he assumes that there issomething wrong with him, the present conscious self. That is, whatever negative behavior occurs is considered a flaw of the present self. While we often pride ourselves for remembering what happened to us in childhood, when it comes to negative memories we are much less willing to look backwards as a cause of our behavior and are more willing to blame our present self for things going wrong. We usually forget all about the person who existed in the past when the faulty belief was created. If this is true, and we believe it is, then it acts as a separate, fractionated personality or possibly many separate personalities. This is often why people will say, "But that wasn't me who did that" or "It's not really like me to think that way." And he is right for it is not the "him" he knows, the conscious, present, middle self. It's a voice stored in the lower self from somewhere in his past, the *Child Within*. The *Child Within* is simply a set of memories, usually negative, that get fixed in time because of the affect on them of the stress mechanism. The child is threatened, or believes himself to be threatened and the mind captures these memories as part of the process of the stress mechanism that holds memories of anything that threaten the individual. These memories are supposed to be for later use in identifying future dangers, however, because of the negative emotions attached to them and the lower self inability to differentiate between the past and the present moment, when it triggers it appears to be acting in the present moment. This process, originally designed to protect the individual, ends up creating pain and threat. The recognition of the faulty belief systems of the negative child within is essential for success in solving problems and creating a new future. The medical profession firmly believes that you can't change people; Huna firmly believes that you can. In truth you can't change people who are either not ready or who don't want to change. Once an individual decides to change, he needs a system that accepts the fact that change is possible and that change provides an easy to use and uncomplicated way of making changes. Most medical doctors are not able to help people change because they don't have the right tools to work with and they don't believe that it can be done. Using the tools we have presented any person can learn how to change themselves.

POSITIVES AND NEGATIVES

When we are born we are omni-potential. While we have genetic direction, that is, our body type and structure is defined and some illnesses, strengths and weaknesses are also defined, the largest part of us, our mind and mental abilities, are open and available to molding. Our ability to be molded beyond our genetics functions on two levels. That which we receive from the outside of us and that which we receive from within us. We are always receiving information and hence being shaped from both all of the time. In fact, each impacts the other. As we process the information we receive from the outside, we make decisions about this information from our beliefs and past experiences. Sometimes we do not have a sufficient sense of ourself or experience to separate that which comes from outside of us and that which comes from within us. The result of this is that while we grow from both our internal and external experiences, we become stinted when we are not able to differentiate between fact and fiction. When, for example, an experience is negative and we accept it as meaning something about us more than it does, we become impacted with a negative charge. Take, for example, a child whose parents tell him at an early age that he is stupid. Since he has bonded with these people and they are necessary for his protection and survival he *expects* everything they tell him to be true. When they tell him that he is stupid, he generally has no frame of reference by which to make an independent judgement, so he accepts their statements as a fact. Since he has no reason to doubt this statement in the beginning he integrates it into his developing self-image. It becomes part of him. After awhile most individuals can't tell the difference between the information they discovered on their own and that which comes from power sources like their parents. These beliefs, once accepted, form the basis of other future belief systems. They are accepted as if they were true and came from his own knowledge of himself. As the years go by he qualifies this belief. That is, he tests it out with his experience of life. Although this initially sounds quite sane, it is not entirely productive since it works both ways. If he truly believes these beliefs, which have frequently been reenforced over and over again in thepast, they may act as a filter for the way he sees the world around him. When something happens that further reinforces these beliefs he may accept it. Therefore, a poor grade on a test, a negative look from a teacher, an unhappy glance from a parent or a disparaging remark from a fellow student, any or all of these could be used as further evidence to support his acceptance of his stupidity.

However, the opposite is also true. Even though some meaningful person told him that he is stupid doesn't mean that he will believe this. He could dismiss such a statement and operate from his own internal knowing. In fact, he can also use the negative comments of others as a driving force to push him forward. He may consider them wrong and set out to look for evidence to demonstrate to himself that he is not stupid or even that he is smart. In such a case the individual doesn't accept the parental statement as fact, but instead, simply as their viewpoint. In such situations he reaches into his internal knowing and operates out of trust in himself. We might ask, "How is it that one individual chooses to go in one direction while another chooses to go in a totally different direction under basically the same circumstances?" No one really knows. It appears that the choice is within the individual all the time. It is possible that his own internal needs or the decisions he makes, even as early as within the uterus, play a large role. It is also possible that the amount of power he confers on his power person or persons (parents, grandparents, sisters, brothers, foster parents, relatives, etc.) makes all of the difference. Whichever it is, isn't important.

What is important however, is that the concept is understood. Then it can be used by the individual him or herself, parents, therapists or other caring persons to overcome poor initial programming. Those who have in the past acted out of their own ignorance, rage or negativity may in the future realize the power they wield on their children and choose to change their ways.

Throughout our development from infancy to adult we are bathed by both positive and negative thought processes and belief systems. Ultimately we must make decisions as to which of these we accept and which we reject. When we accept more negative than positive ideas either from an external source our from our own internal belief system, we can end up in what might be called a *negative mindset*. Conversely, by accepting more positive than negative ideas we may end up in a *positive mindset*. When many of these negative thought processes are linked to the body, to physical processes or to emotions, one end result can be illness. While this is not the only way illness occurs, it is certainly a common way. Negative belief systems are also at the root of a great deal of human misery. They may also underlie social problems such as failure syndromes, poor job performance, divorce, broken marriages, child abuse, addictions, criminal behavior and much more. The basic mechanism working here is *negative programming* of the individual. Not unlike the way we program a computer, we are programmed as well. When someones programming is more negative than positive this can diminish this individual's potential and capacity for achievement.

We generally refer to belief systems which undermine the individual as *Faulty Belief Systems*. They are faulty because they are not true for this individual. They take him away not only from his own potential but from what he can do for others. Huna suggests that thoughts have substance, form and shape and since they are made of energy they are *real and material*. The Huna master, therefore considered beliefs to be physical objects that act on us to bring about what we ask for. Since they are real they can act positively or negatively. They can be transported, stored, contained and nurtured. Since they are matter they cannot be destroyed. They can, however, be transformed. What this tells us is that we cannot destroy these negative or faulty belief systems no matter how hard we try. According to the Huna master, once a thought is created all you can do is transformit or replace it with a new, more healthy thought. If you feed a thought (with your life energy, *mana*) it will grow and dominate your thinking. Dwelling on a specific thought directs power to that thought. As you do this, two things happen: you empower the thought and you become accustomed to it. When a thought is empowered it begins to take precedence over all other thoughts. The more power given it, the higher its ranking. For example, depression often occurs because the individual gives power to thoughts that are negatively structured. "I can't do it." "I am useless." "I am getting nowhere." "I am stupid." "Why would anyone want me as their friend?" "I hate myself." When these negative thoughts continue for an extended period of time, more and more power is given to them and the individual begins believe them and as he believes them they rob him of life energy and he eventually begins to feel depressed. Soon he has less and less energy, his life becomes boring and he feels worthless. His may lose interest in his job and stay up all night watching television. As he sees people being happy and succeeding he may say to himself, "They have it all and I have nothing." "Life is really not worth living." "Maybe I am better off dead."

If this line of thought continues unabated, the process may lead to chronic depression. It could even lead to hospitalization. It could also lead to dropping out, to taking jobs below the individual's capacities, to bad relationships, to a poor work record, to failing at many of the things the person does, to low self-esteem, to a poor self-image, and a wasted life. It can and does, in some situations, lead to suicide. Most frequently we see it leading to stress, disease and illness through the stress mechanism. Often such individuals develop some kind of illness which if not reversed can lead to chronic disease or even death. Death is often through mechanisms such as heart disease (a broken heart) or some metabolic disease (out of balance) or cancer (something eating him up alive). It is also not unusual to see the progressing toward alcoholism, injury or disability. Sometimes it just persists for years, smoldering in the form of anger, rage, abusiveness or apathy.

THE ROLE OF SIN IN ILLNESS

The Huna master recognizes that not only faulty beliefs and lies play a major role in creating conflict and illness, also the sins or hurts that we have done to ourselves and others, as well as the sins we believe we have committed, all play major roles in creating illness. Each sin is a block or complex that undermines the lower self - middle self relationship. Sins create a negative self image which leads to stress, and in doing so, it sabotages all of the other good works we do. When we are aware of the sins we have committed we can cleanse ourself. However, when we are unaware of them or have created sins that are unremovable, we ultimately suffer from them. (See the section on Cleansing Sin.)

WHAT IS SIN?

When we use the word *sin*, it may seem as though we have suddenly switched from a discussion of healing medical illnesses to a discussion of healing spiritual illnesses. This, however, is not the case. We use words such as *hurt, lies, faulty belief systems* or *conflicts* interchangeably to represent the same basic concepts. No matter which word is used, the basics are the same; sins represent lies that we either do to ourself or accept about ourself or about others. Sins, since they are lies, create conflicts in our life. Sins, lies and conflicts often diminish us, in our own eyes. They act as a negative force or "power" to undermine us or to drive us in the wrong direction. Once a sense of conflict is perceived by our mind, the stress mechanism is triggered and we enter into a state of siege where we are both the attacker and the victim. We are no longer our own self, happily going about our business and marching toward our highest and best self. We are diverted and distracted away from who we really are. As we explained earlier, this process can eventually lead to SRD's. In fact, it is likely that most SRD's are most commonly created through this mechanism. Feelings of sin create conflict and trigger the stress mechanism. They cause us pain and harm us. We stated earlier that in Huna sins only occur when we have caused intentional hurt to our self or to others. However, in most Western religions, there are many sins many of which have nothing to do with causing hurt or harm to anyone. In our Western world simply believing in sin can lead to creating sins which can cause us problems. This is the bind of modern religion. Through believing in sin, we commit a sin. Through believing in retribution, we cause harm and therefore once again commit a sin. If we accept the concept that sin is all around us or that violating any small rule is sinful then it would seem to follow that this would create a lot of disease in the world. And, in fact, there is a great deal of disease in this world. Can we eliminate disease by eliminating sin? The answer to this question has more to do with what we consider to be the sins then anything else. Stated slightly differently, the number of lies, faulty belief systems and conflicts that we and others create in our life. *If we were to eliminate most sin, would we eliminate most disease?* To find out if this is really true, we would have to do just exactly that; eliminate all or most sins that presently exist. However, we all know that this is not going to happen, at least not in the forseeable future. There is, however, much that we can do. We can eliminate all extraneous and unnecessary sin from our own life and see what happens. To accomplish this, the simplest thing we can do is to accept the Huna definition of sin as *the intentional hurt of another*, and then work carefully and diligently to keep from hurting others.

REMOVING SINS

Modern medicine has no real way of dealing with "sin" or guilt. One can spend years and years in psychotherapy trying to undo the emotional destruction caused by even simple sins or guilt over relatively inconsequential matters. Possibly even worse, modern medicine, as advanced as it is, continues to allow certain religions to essentially inundate their believers with "sin consciousness." Under these circumstances one might wonder how modern this medicine really is. Since in Huna the only sin is *the intentional hurt of another (or ones self)* it has no such problem . From a health standpoint the concept of a single sin combines all of the Ten Commandments into one Commandment. This leaves the individual with a clear sense of what is right and wrong. *If you intentionally or deliberately do or say something that hurts or causes another person pain or suffering then what you have done is wrong and you have sinned.* We realize that many people brought up in a Christian-Judaic household might consider this to be much too simple and even misleading. However, the concept of sin in the Christian-Judaic system is much too complicated. In fact, as many people brought up in these teachings might admit, virtually everything a person does can have an element of sin within it. Possibly the only thing that doesn't would be an act or action that doesn't hurt another. However, this could be qualified in so many different ways that it, too, is likely to end up with some sin attached to it. The belief behind this single sin concept is that the individual who causes *intentional* hurt to another diminishes himself and therefore hurts himself. He will always know that he has done this and the consequences of his actions will fall back upon him to cause loss of what he wants *most* in his life. This doesn't happen because he is simply a bad person but rather because he knows that he has done wrong and that his guilt, shame and disgust in himself deprecates him and makes him unworthy of what he really wants in life. When an individual asks for something through prayer (which in a sense is always the way we ask for things in our life), the memory and associated guilt of having hurt another will likely block the ability of the lower self to ask for it because it will not feel worthy.

In Huna philosophy the individual who has sinned can always be released from that sin by performing a number of actions. He can make up the damage he caused to the other individual, he can apologize and have his apology accepted by the person he injured or he can do something for the general good. This means he can give of himself or his possessions in such a way that his intentional misdoing is paid for. He can give to charity, to the community or to a family member of the person he hurt, for example. In the process of giving a *sacrifice,* he cleanses himself. If the sacrifice is accepted, he is set free and can become healthy again. If the sacrifice is insufficient or is not given in the true spirit of undoing his wrong deed, he willnot be freed and he will be left carrying the sin with him. In this sense, Huna is protective not only of the individual but of the group as well.

One might ask what about morality. In Huna, morality is an issue between two people. If no person is hurt, no moral rules are violated. Certainly, as in our society, no one is protected against the psychopath, the individual who has no sense of right or wrong, no sense of other. Typically the psychopath doesn't see his intentional hurt of others as either intentional or hurtful. He can justify himself through some form of bizarre thinking that allows him not to have feelings of guilt, shame or sin. These individuals are outside of almost every system except the law. Whether psychopaths existed in Hawaii or Polynesia is not completely clear. There is evidence that they may well have existed but this is not really an issue, since psychopaths are an aberration in any society. What is important, is what goes on inside of the average individual, the everyday person like you and me. We are the ones in this society who suffer from the multiplicity of sins that exist in our society and the lack of a system of forgiveness and redemption. While it may seem that we are confusing religion with medicine in this discussion, let me assure you that we are not. Our present society separates these two aspects of the individual. But Huna clearly demonstrates that they are not easily separated without ultimately creating disease and illness.

While many people would like to see religion and science separated, this is in truth an impossibility. The key here is that many religions have become an infinite source of dogmas, most of which have a minimal sense of reality to man as he truly is. While it is true that they may seek the truth of man's spiritual nature, few find it and many distort it. The modern generations of physicians generally choose to ignore the destructive elements of many of today's religious groups. For centuries the medical profession has adopted a *live and let live* policy. However, if wellness is the goal, this is certainly not in anyone's best interest. This is not to suggest that medicine should revolt against religion. But there should be a reality check when a patient comes to his physician with illnesses that are directly related to distorted beliefs in his own sins and the sins of others. The Huna oriented physician can truly say to the patient, "Did you intentionally act to hurt someone?" If the patient's answer is yes, the physician can ask, "How do you plan to make it up to him, apologize and resolve this problem?" If the answer is no, then his question to his patient should be, "Why are you using it against yourself if you had no intention to hurt another?" Once the intention is established, the physician can help his patient problem-solve his way back to health and well-being. He can reassure him that his guilt, pain and suffering is unnecessary. If these feelings persist he can help him to set up a program of forgiveness. I realize that this approach sounds more like the role of the clergy but in a sense the physician is the clergy for the mind and the body. If the physician feels that he is not capable of solving problems and of helping his patient regain his self-love and self-esteem then he should be able to refer his patient to someone who can. This could be either a Huna-based physician or a clergy who is not deterred from healing by the dogma of his church. The physician also must be a realist. If the patient doesn't want to get well, there is very little he can do for him *except* care about him enough to tell him the truth. If the physician is unable to let go of his dogma about the separation of medicine from the spiritual aspect of his patient, hopefully the patient will seek out a new physician.

GUILT

On several occasions we have brought up the concept of guilt. Often many of us have difficulty with guilt that we hold from our past, from our childhood and from our plans for the future. What is guilt? Guilt can be defined from many different perspectives. The definition we will use is somewhat simplified. We feel however, that it is applicable most of the time when we are working with people who experience guilt. Guilt is *our inability to love ourself.* This definition holds no matterwhat the reason for our guilt is. Most frequently, guilt occurs when we take responsibility for an action, decision or feeling that either hurts someone or we believe hurts someone. This harm can be caused either purposely or non-purposely. Guilt, as you will see, is an important aspect of creating problems which keep us from getting what we want out of life. Feelings of guilt contribute to the reason that most people feel unworthy and undeserving of what they desire in life. The reason that we define guilt in terms of love is that love stimulates our body, our immune system and our ability to feel worthy of getting what we want out of life. Those of us who work with the healing systems of the body generally recognize that a loss of self-love is frequently associated with health problems, illness and a decline in the quality of life.

Love is the protector, it innervates the immune system and maintains it. When self-love falters, the healing and immune systems begin to break down. As it declines further the initial microscopic failures turn to cracks and snags. As time passes and self-love fails, more and more breakdowns may occur until whole organ systems begin to fail and disease and chronic disease occur. We see this all around us as systems and organizations, machines and societies fail for lack of upkeep or proper attention, because of neglect and, not infrequently, due to sabotage. The village which is abandoned is soon claimed by the jungle. The neighborhood not cared for soon decays. So it is with the immune system. If you do not love yourself, you begin a process of breakdown. Think about it in a practical sense. When you value your car you take care of it. The more you value it, the more careful and loving your attention. You are more likely to wash it, park it in the safest areas, have it serviced regularly, rotate its tires, check the water and oil and drive more carefully. The less you value it, the more likely you are to ignore it, forgetting to lube it, change the oil or provide regular maintenance. Because you don't value it enough to protect it, it is ultimately more likely to break down from lack of care. Wear and tear will be greater and it will deteriorate more rapidly. When you are unable to love yourself you also take less care of yourself. You may eat more junk foods, higher cholesterol foods, get less exercise and let yourself get run down. You may not reach for your highest and best self, look for loving relationships or work at the job you really want. Because you are doing less than the best for yourself, the message you give to your immune system is, "I deserve less (possibly much less) than the best from you." Hence, the immune system (as well as other bodily systems) perform at a lower level than it is capable of. You may subjectively be aware of this as you experience episodes of recurrent upper respiratory illnesses or mild bacterial and viral infections. Eventually, as self-love and value diminish, various types of illnesses and problems occur. Alcoholism, excessive smoking, gambling or overeating all may suggest that there is a significant breach in self-love and self-value. With loss of self-love and self-value come changes in the way the individual eats and sleeps, his personal hygiene, and his self-image. Over time the immune system may significantly malfunction and allow cancer or chronic diseases to develop or even a self-willed death through illness or accident.

Diminishment of self-love and self-value occurs in other ways. For example, when we commit sins. In the setting of the Christian-Judaic tradition most of us find ourselves eventually committing one sin or another. With each sin comes a measure of guilt. One doesn't have to even commit a major sin to end up having a great deal of guilt. A small sin, something rather innocuous, can lead to significant guilt feelings. Guilt adversely affects the immune system as it suggests that we have *become unworthy, diminished and less loveable.* The entire concept of guilt is to feel bad about ourselves, to feel tarnished and lessened. Listen to the message it gives to our lower self and to our immune system, "I am guilty of a crime (against societal/religious laws) and deserve to be punished. I am unworthy of love and anything good. I deserve to burn in hell (to get ill, to be in pain) in order to be cleansed and freed of my sins." Notice the hidden messages which while not said or thought are built into our societal history and essence. No wonder we have a society which is full of illness.

Fear is often the consequence of guilt. If you believe that you have sinned and that there must be some sort of retribution for your sins then you must live in fear until this retribution (even if it is from the self) is complete. However, we generally do not see illness as an act which we have responsibility for. We usually see it as an outside force unrelated to ourselves, our decisions, guilt, fears and faulty beliefs. Because of this, illness may occur but guilt is not released. While we commonly hear people say, "I know this sickness is a punishment," few really take this seriously as they also believe that sickness comes from outside of them. Therefore, their illness does not release them from their sins and the fear is not relieved. Fear may actually increase because of the fear generated by the illness. The process, then, continues until, as we described above, it reaches a critical level.

The Huna concept of only one sin, *the intentional hurt of another or ourself*, greatly reduces all possibility of sinning down to a premeditated crime for it to cause problems for ourself. Hence, guilt can be greatly diminished or even eliminated. Self-love and self-value can continue to flourish and the immune system can be energized positively. Huna has recognized the importance of self-love. The process of healing requires that <u>all</u> complexes, fears, guilt and sense of sin be eliminated. We will discuss the exact mechanism used to accomplish this in a later section. Guilt is an insidious killer and, at all costs, must be eliminated. Recognizing what we have stated above is an excellent first step. The next step is to make amends and release all guilt.

SECTION III

USING HUNA TO HEAL

CHAPTER ONE

The Role of Huna in Healing Illness

HEALING ENERGIES

In Interventive Medicine the physician makes the decisions. He prescribes the treatment. As the source of energy for the patient, he empowers the healing and in doing so he takes this power away from his patient. Healing requires energy. Even taking medications requires energy. When there is no energy healing will be inefficient and when all energy is gone we have death.

THE THREE ENERGIES OF THE BODY

Huna, unlike Western medicine, recognizes three types of energies. They are *mana, mana-mana* and *Mana-Loa*. Huna teaches how to find and use these energies. The Huna master tells us that these energies of healing are the same energies as our life force. They surround us and are part of our being all of the time and as long as we are alive. These energies can be expended, transformed and regenerated but they can never be destroyed.

Mana: The Huna masters called the primary energy, *mana*. It is the energy of the lower self. It is created by the interaction of the food we eat and the oxygen we breathe. It is our *life force*. Mana is an energy of a low vibrational nature. It is essential for the maintenance and day-to-day operation of our body. Without it we would be unable to operate, we would become cold and we would die. One might compare mana to electricity. Just as electricity runs our home and our city, mana energizes us. Mana exists within us only while we live and it is lost from us when we die. It runs our biologic functions and is the source of energy for our muscles. It provides us with the ability to work, live life and ultimately heal ourselves. It is the energy of the stress mechanism as well.

Mana-Mana: This is the energy of the conscious self or *will power*. In Hawaiian, when a word is doubled it signifies that it is greater than its original form. So it is with mana-mana which has greater energyand is of a higher vibrational nature than mana. The mana-mana of the conscious self is stronger then mana alone but it still cannot get to the Higher Self. It too starts as energy produced by eating and breathing. Will power is important, not because it powers biologic functions, but because it powers our desires and intentional actions. Without will power we would have no way of getting what we want in life. Whenever you reach for something you desire this motion is driven by will power, whenever you want something and go after it you are using will power. Mana-mana is the tool of the conscious self and allows us to have free will. While mana works entirely for the good of the individual, mana-mana, being related to the will and thoughts of the individual, can have both positive and negative components. While mana is well directed at the level of the lower self, with its basic programming coming from our genetics and biology, it can be affected directly by commands from the middle self, mana-mana and hence can be indirectly affected by what we want and what we think. Hence it is also under the effect of our illusions and our greed.

The power of the middle self, mana-mana, can be either broad in its context or narrow sighted. As will or desire, it can be mixed with emotions and react to internal feelings and emotions long forgotten by conscious memory. It can act on the lower self either as a benevolent friend or as a demi-god force, out of its own belief and in its own cause.

Mana-Loa: The third energy is Mana-Loa. It is the energy of the Higher Self and is often thought about as the psychic energy or the spiritual energy. Mana-loa is said to be at a vibrational level which is higher than either mana or mana-mana. While Western medicine hardly recognizes such forms of energy it is clear that mana-loa plays an important role in our life. Mana-loa, being the energy of the Higher Self, acts differently than either of the other two energies. It is involved in prayer, including healing and desiring prayers as well as connecting us to the Intelligent Universe we live in. Through the process of Huna prayer mana-mana, as will power, commitment or decision, is sent to the lower self. If the lower self is willing to accept the prayer and is not blocked by complexes, fear or guilt then mana is activated and sent through the connection (the *Aka cord* discussed in the next section) from the lower self to the Higher Self. When the prayer is accepted by the Higher Self, mana-loa is activated and creates what was asked for in the Huna prayer. Occasionally, the lower self may recognizes a *higher truth* (one which may or may not be seen by the conscious self) and it lets this truth in to its level of consciousness. It may become immediately energized by its own positive emotions, i.e., the passion of being. A doorway opens (acceptance, self-love or letting go) and spontaneous enlightenment can occur. When this happens mana is involuntarily sent up to the Higher Self, mana-loa is produced and healing takes place. Generally, this occurs while we are caught up in a problem that needs to be solved, but it can also happen while at rest when nothing at all is happening.

The Huna master believes strongly in the concept of prayer, he believes that through prayer we can literally have anything we want in the Universe. Using prayer and mana-loa the Huna master can heal, he can change the weather, communicate with animals, with spirits and telepathically. He can also use his connection to the Intelligent Universe to know the future, see the past, as well as hear and see at a distance. While the mere mention of these abilities often frightens or revolts a Western scientist, the Huna master knows them as everyday conditions that can be taught or learned by anyone who would merely open his or her mind to the possibility. In Western science and medicine these abilities are denied and hence, never really understood. Since charlatans often claim to have such powers, and when an individual comes along who can use the powers of mana-loa, he or she is often classified as a fraud.

The recognition of these three energies is extremely important for when they are abused, as they often are, energy is drawn from the lower and middle selves and the individual may complain that he has "no energy," that he is "fatigued" or even depressed. It isn't that he really has "no energy,"but instead, his energies have been misdirected or drawn off into useless tasks such as worrying, suppressing fears or anxieties, or coping with anger. Energy is being used to deal with emotional conflicts which have been created, manifested as stress, fear and tension, instead of being directed to healing and enlivening where it belongs. When an individual is feeling limited he allocates his energy poorly. Energy, which should be used to activate the immune system, for example, may be misdirected into worrying about a problem that he is fearful of solving. Energy can also be drawn away from the *will to live* and the zest for life. Since Western medicine has no attachment to or understanding of the role of life force energy, persons with energy problems are often diagnosed as suffering from chronic fatigue, anxiety, immune system deficiency or depression. Physicians look for viruses or other physical conditions as a potential cause and, when none is found, they tell their patients that it is all in their head, they treat them with mood elevators or uppers or ignore them entirely. In the end the real cause is missed. If, as in the case of so called Epstein-Barr disease, a virus is incriminated as a cause of this chronic fatigue and lowered resistance, scientists find themselves unable to agree because the complex is sovaried and the loss of energy so profound that many scientists cannot agree that a single virus can create all of the varying patterns seen in practice. When abnormal findings are noted, instead of recognizing the underlying dynamics and appreciating the symptoms as a sign of the misdirection of the body's energy, a *disease syndrome* is looked for. Ultimately, the problem is attributed to a cause which is outside of the person. One which may well in reality be a secondary invader allowed in by the body after it lost its ability to control its own biologic functions, the immune system, the antibody-antigen system and the many layers of defensive systems that normally protect us. Since all of these systems are under the control of the lower self, once its vital energies are drawn off or misdirected, its ability to control, run and maintain efficiency over the body's many defensive systems is accordingly diminished. Physicians, who have been trained to look for a cause outside of us have great difficulty tuning into the real underlying causes and hence their patients suffer and often go years, or even throughout their entire lifetime, without help or cure. Since the medical profession generally ignores the existence of this life force energy, there is no way to use its positive healing forces and creativity in healing. A physician might observe that a specific patient has staying power or vitality but he misses the fact that the patient not only generates it from within but he also can control it and use it for healing.

We often see the effects of this life force energy in healers as well as in "powerful men and women" who seem to have boundless energies to accomplish things. While we think of the energy of the middle self principally as will power and action, it can also be thought of as motion and function and getting results. Hence, while we think of the strength generated by this energy as an important aspect of getting things done in life we can also think of it as play and having fun.

There is, however, another side to these forces for they can also be recognized as having to do with the dark side of the force. The Huna master will be quick to tell you that any force which is enjoyed and used for good can also be used for evil. Both sides exist simultaneously. Both are simply paths chosen by the individual to which he directs his power. The Huna master understands that these energies and the power that accompany them are indeed neutral. They have no direction. No sense of right or wrong, no sense of goodness or decency or evil. These directions are created by the middle or lower self or the two working together. One area which is rarely thought about in Western Medicine is the use of mana-loa, spiritual strength, for healing. The medical profession often puts this down as hocus pocus, that is until they have expended **all** of their efforts to no avail. Then, when there is nothing more to do, nothing more to offer, the physician will say that it is now *entirely* in God's hands (considering this to be some other, more powerful force, greater and stronger than himself with skills greater than those of medical science.)

Huna, on the other hand, uses these three energies (mana, mana-mana and *Mana-Loa*) quite differently. They are used as an integral part of healing. In fact, as far as the Huna master is concerned there can be no healing without them. The first level of healing is mana. As we have stated earlier it provides the energy to maintain the body's defensive systems. If the individual has properly directed the lower self to be on guard and is directing sufficient energy to the protective mechanisms, the individual is unlikely to get sick in the first place. All of the work of the lower self and its mana exist at a level below that of the awareness of the individual himself. Hence, he does not have to watch it, constantly energize it or actively maintain it. The second tier of the lower self and mana in healing is the immediate response of the body if a microorganism or parasite does penetrate its outer defenses. In this case the lower self has several offensive mechanisms available to it. Once again these mechanisms are powered by mana. These offensive systems rush to the area of invasion and meet the enemy to destroy it. In the third tier we have the stress system itself. Whenever a threat occurs which exceeds the capacity of the many layers of the defensive and offensive systems as we have just discussed, the stress mechanism is invoked. Once again mana is the energy of the stress mechanism which is basically a biologic function managed by the lower self. Mana also provides the energy of movement to get us away from danger and to move us towards safety. It is also the energy of procreation and the energy that helps us to find food. Lastly, man is the energy of the healing and repair systems of the body. These functions, mediated by the lower self, generally require no work on our part. If we are cut the body knows what to do to heal the wound. While we often seek help from the doctor, who cleans, dresses and even sutures the would, it is still the lower self, using mana, which performs the healing.

The use of mana-mana in protecting and healing is also essential. Will is important to making decisions that keep us out of trouble and protect us. When threatened, the stress mechanism is triggered, but without mana-mana, the individual may not have heart or strength to fully defend himself. Mana-mana is necessary to get him to the hospital, if injured, as well as form the will to live once there. The role of mana-loa is one that is unclear to most Western physicians. Because of confusion over the role of religion in healing, areas such as psychic healing, healing at a distance and spontaneous healing, often thought of as miracles, are often quite confusing to the Western physician. With an understanding of Huna many of the misconceptions associated with these types of healing can be cleared up. These types of healing require more than just mana-loa, they require an interaction of mana, mana-mana and mana-loa to perform the healing prayers which petition the Higher Self to create immediate healing. The role of mana-loa along with the other forms of energy will be discussed in greater detail in a later section about Huna prayer.

BREATH AND HEALING

In Huna, not unlike Eastern Medical philosophy, breathing has great value. It is important from both the scientific and spiritual perspectives.

Scientifically, breathing imparts the following benefits:

     a) Cleanses system, removes toxic materials from the bloodstream
     b) Brings in oxygen, generating energy to burn food
     c) Reduces stress
     d) Works muscles of the chest, diaphragm and abdomen
     e) Increases blood flow to the heart
     f) Increases oxygen circulation throughout the body
     g) Increases oxygen to the brain
     h) Improves blood sugar utilization

These and other functions of the respiratory system and the process of breathing have been taughtin most medical schools. However, what the physician is not taught is how to connect breathing with helping and healing his patients through its connection to the generation of body energy (mana and mana-mana) and spiritual healing energy (mana-loa). The Huna practitioner uses supercharged energy to directly heal, to return the physical system to energy harmony and balance, and to overcome problems of blocked energy. He makes use of it in prayer (not religious prayer but

Huna prayer) which will be discussed in a later section. The production of energy is regulated carefully by the body. Not all energy is produced or utilized at once. Significant portions are stored. The physiologist would say that when food is ingested not all of it is used immediately. Part of it is transformed into glycogen and then stored as fat. The storage of fat represents the wisdom of the body to prepare ahead for possible emergencies due to stresses such as fasting, famine or for long periods of increased energy needs. When the body needs immediate energy, glycogen is released from the liver and enters into a process of metabolic breakdown which transforms it into glucose, blood sugar. When liver glycogen drops below a critical level a message is sent to the fat storage areas and fat is released into the blood stream to make new glycogen to replenish its stores as well as blood sugar levels. Once released into the blood stream, blood sugar is acted on by oxygen, brought into the lungs by breath and then stored and transported to where it is needed in red blood cells. This oxygen joins with the blood sugar to create an internal fire which burns the glucose and releases energy into the system as mana to be utilized as needed by the lower self. The quality of the fuel available is of great importance. Since oxygen is always oxygen, the most important factor then becomes eating a diet. That is, a diet that provides not only necessary foods but all other essential elements (vitamins, minerals and other essential nutrients) required for the precise functioning of the lower self. Proper breathing and the ability to direct the breathing process is also imperative to the production of energy.

ENERGY AND HEALING

These processes give us the force and energy that we need for the work that we must do. The nicest part of it is that we generally do not have to attend to these processes. They are handled automatically by the lower self. However, if the lower self becomes bound up in conflicts or malfunctions from excessive stress, these energies can be misdirected. In Huna, as in the Eastern philosophy, breathing is significant, not only its biologic processes but also because of its other effects on the body, the mind and the spirit. Breathing is an element the Huna practitioner looks at early in the process of evaluation of the individual. The way one breathes, the depth of breath and the breathing pattern can all be clues. The old family doctor understood this and would often first watch the breathing of his patient. From this he would learnwhether his patient was really sick and with what type of illness. He could often discern other factors such as to gauge his patients level of anxiety, whether his patient was telling the truth, whether he was fearful and much more. In medical school, and later in practice, I found that the modern physician knows little if anything about these clues. In fact, breathing is generally ignored except in the most extreme situations such as shock or in conditions such as asthma when it is important to determine the immediate status of his patient or the effect of medications given.

For most people breathing is not recognized as consequential except when they are involved in some form of athletics where breathing and controlling the breath can make a significant difference in performance and ability to function. Breath also becomes a major issue when it is lost, such as after a fall, a blow to the head, abdomen or chest, or during drowning. Years ago, in learning how to scuba dive, I found out about the power of breath when the instructor said, "Before you jump into the water you must remember one thing, don't forget to breathe." Generally, we have a natural instinct to hold your breath when we put our head under water. This instinct is extremely strong. During in my first lesson, I did forget, I held my breath and when I finally did breathe I almost choked on the sudden rush of air from the scuba equipment.

Few serious runners have not experienced the so called "second wind," a phenomenon that occurs after the runner reaches a point of feeling extremely fatigued and about at the end of his ability. He takes a deep breath and suddenly a new vitality floods into him. Newly energized, his stamina and his capacity to run soar. This occurrence is not unfamiliar to the Huna practitioner who sees this as a function of the lower self in generating a new level of energy because of the intention and desire of the individual to persist in what he is doing. The individual who doesn't like running, who is bored or uninterested will almost never experience this second wind unless he has a need to go beyond his limits. This energy is part of the process the Huna practitioner uses to heal and be healed. It is this energy that the person who desires healing must find and bring to himself to promote healing. The "second wind," while most commonly associated with running, is not really a function of running or physical effort, but rather a function of intention and desire. As the runner reaches the point where he *feels* he is at the end of his capacity, fatigued to his limit and about ready to give up, he makes a leap of intention and pushes that extra bit to take that next and, possibly, last step. At this point with the next breath, mana, the lower level energy is created. Of course, as you might suspect the second wind experience also includes mana-mana (will power). The runner must want to go further, he must want to continue to run. This will to run is sent to the lower self as an image, a message, or an intention, to go to the limit of capacity. This desire and the combination of the intention and activation of mana power invokes the production of mana-loa, the supreme energy of the Higher

Self, in a sense a Huna Prayer is created. This same process, unrelated to running of course, occurs with immediate healing. Whatwe have described is the basis of all miracles and all healing.

The Huna master learns to bring this energy up at will, he also learns that once it is generated it can be used by him to perform all kinds of tasks, the most important of which is healing. So powerful is this energy that renegade Huna practitioners, that is practitioners of the art of *ana-ana*, the death prayer, at times would use this energy not to heal but to kill. The capacity of this energy when used by a trained Huna master for healing is astounding. However, one of the most significant values of this energy is that it is also available to be used by all of us as well. In its simplest form it comes from eating good, healthy foods and breathing normally. In its higher forms it can be attained easily by learning certain simple skills, breathing exercises, that teach us how to breathe to maximize the intake of oxygen and the distribution of the energy formed from it. While the ancient healers knew that the breath is an important key to health and healing, their lessons have been lost on present day lifestyles. The power of breathing requires a book of its own and is only a portion of what must be considered by the individual looking for healing. Of equal importance is what you *think* when you breathe. Forming a clear, concise image of what you desire, and the intention to make it happen empowers the Higher Self to materialize what you ask for. If what we think is meaningless or confused then what you get will also be meaningless andconfused. If what you ask for is negative, or will cause intentional or even secondary harm or hurt to another, the Huna master knows that the negative request will return negativity to your life. There are many stories of ancient Huna practitioners, some very powerful masters, who misused their powers, in the end, as the old adage goes, "He who lives by the sword dies by the sword," all regretted it. It is important to remember that Huna power is based on the "no harm" rule. Creating hurt or harm to another is a sin and no power on earth will protect those that use Huna powers to cause intentional harm or hurt to another. While modern medicine has little interest in what we, as the patient, think, the Huna practitioner is aware that what you think creates the substance of your life as well as all of the events that surround you. If you are not aware of this fact, it will be very hard to accept that what you get in life is created by you. The unenlightened individual tends to project what he gets in life outside of himself. "Someone else is responsible, not me." With this point of view, we feel powerless, as if some other powerful forces control us, our life and our destiny, while all the time it is our thoughts and beliefs which control these powerful forces.

As a medical practitioner I often see individuals who literally talk themselves into being sick. I also see individuals who talk themselves out of being sick. I am often amazed at the power of themind in creating illness and in healing illness. The combination of our thoughts and the power that we generate in our life are often the deciding factors of how our life turns out. To a degree, probably all of us know this but we are often talked out of this belief by skeptical people around us and, unfortunately, even by our medical doctors. Understanding the role of our own energy production and utilization can help us greatly to clarify the reasons why we get ill and how we heal ourselves. What we think can and does act directly on our defensive and immune systems as well as on our healing systems. This is not some random occurrence, or something that happens by accident but rather a well designed plan of the creator of the body, mind and spirit, the Intelligence of the Universe. We could say, if we desire, that it is part of nature's way of doing things. The powers we have described above work to heal as well as to destroy. This is obvious from what we know about the world around us. We seem to clearly understand man's capacity to do evil, if we could only understand and then master our ability to heal then we would be living in an entirely different world.

GETTING WHAT WE WANT FROM OUR LIFE

In the end, energy is nothing but an aspect of our mental attitude. We generate it. First wegenerate it with our mind, then we concentrate it and finally, we focus it. We can use it to build, we can use it for performing tasks and for working. We can use it creatively or we can use it to destroy and break down things around us. If we are not aware of what we are doing, the energy can be directed uselessly or negatively. Without our direction it is simply undifferentiated and useless energy. One of the major problems that we, as energetic creatures have, is generating and directing sufficient ongoing energy to maintain what we have built. If we create something and then redirect our life energy in an entirely different direction, the former will begin to decay. This often happens with our work, our hopes and dreams. We initially create them out of a desire to better ourselves, or out of some fantasy for our future, and then we abandon them, leaving them without the energy to accomplish what we wanted in the first place. Later, we ask ourselves, "Where did our dreams go and what happened to our goals of so many years ago." On the other hand, when we desire something and we put our energy into it we usually accomplish it. This is true whether the goal is positive or negative. Unfortunately, this can also happen when we don't really want what we desired. Take the student who is so afraid of failing that he puts all his energy into preparing to fail or creating reasons why he will fail. If there is not enough of him that wants to be successful he will ultimately create his own failure. Taking in the limitless energy of the Universe and then focusing this *mana* through breathing and eating, we can generate enormous amounts of energy. This energy can quickly add to our sense of well-being and it can also be used to make our dreams and desires come true. The lower self, essentially being a robot, can take this energy and shape our life using the blueprints we have created through our thoughts, plans and desires. To do this, it steps up the voltage of this energy to a level or frequency which matches the creative energy of the Universe.

In Huna the thoughts we create are considered to be material objects and are referred to as *thought-forms*. These thought-forms were referred to by the Huna practitioners as *seeds*. The understanding of this was stated in the Bible: "As you sow, so shall you reap." The meaning here is clear. The seeds (and thoughts) that you have planted give you what you wanted. The problem, of course, is that many of us are not aware of this and we are surprised at what we get. In Huna these seeds are created by the middle self, nurtured by the lower self which maintains them and preserves them, and are vitalized by the Higher Self and its high energy. They are then returned fully developed or materialized for our use and development. All this we already know for the farmer who plants corn seeds expects a corn plant to grow from them. The soil and his hard work nurture and protect it until the corn unfolds, almost as if by an act of God. The farmer than chooses what he wishes with his corn. He can eat it, give it away or grind it up and use it forflour. As the production of energy is also tied to our diet, to the types and the quality of the foods we eat and the substances they contain so is our ultimate power. Often, when we eat "junk foods", not only do we not get enough energy from these foods but our body is required to use the little energy left in it to burn them up. Today's foods are often deficient in vitamins and minerals and eating less than nourishing foods can end up diminishing the energy needed to heal ourselves and maintain our health and well-being.

BLOCKING OUR DESIRES

Since the lower self acts like a robot, it will do whatever the middle self tells it to do. The more the middle self believes in what it is asking for and the greater the power of the will, the more the lower self will believe that the action is proper. This is true unless complexes, blocks or faulty belief systems already exist. When a complex clashes with an immediate order a **conflict** is set up. In such situations the lower self will resist the new order or thought and may end up responding differently than what was desired or expected of it. Generally, however, these blocks and conflicts occur below the awareness of the middle self. When the middle self is aware, it can change its instructions or orders in some way so that no conflict occurs and, therefore, no complex or blocks are activated. Complexes are formed when instructions that are given are not in the best interest of the individual. That is, when they ultimately impair survival, act as a threat or create conflict which deters the individual from its evolutionary path. A complex or block can be created in several ways. For example, when the middle self gives an order or instruction which is in direct conflict with biological programming. Another example is when the middle self gives an order to do something and the individual is hurt or threatened as a result. The lower self will create a memory of the outcome, and whenever the same order or one the lower self judges to be similar, it either refuses to take the action or does something which it deems safer and less in conflict. A third way that blocks are formed is when trauma occurs to us. For example as we discussed earlier, the young woman who was molested had her problems dealing with men later in life.

Complexes are also caused by *lies* that we give power to. Lies are also faulty belief systems. They work against the healthy self. They are often heard within our head as thoughts, or as words, pictures or simply as a "knowing."[12] We call this voice that we hear in our head that is lying to us, the *Dialogue Voice*. It differs from the voice of truth which we also hear and know to be true. We call this the *Core Voice*. By definition the core voice always tells us the truth, while the dialogue voice always lies to us. Since both are really only our own thoughts, we may often have great difficulty distinguishing which is which. Is the voice we hear the truth or is it a lie? Generally, we can only tell the difference between them by our own experiences with them. To recognize which is which, we must get in touch with our feelings, past experiences and our instincts. As we follow our thoughts and we try to hear which voice we have been listening to and we correlate our beliefs with our life experiences. It eventually becomes easier and easier to recognize when we are telling ourselves the truth and when we are lying to ourselves. Simply said, it is a matter of practice. Complexes are formed from the lies of the middle self and its dialogue voice these complexes are then turned around by the lower self and used to protect us. A case history may help to give us an example of how it all works:

> Bruce had been abused by his father when he was a child. His father would shout orders at him and demand his immediate compliance. At some point Bruce's dialogue voice told him that,

not only his father but *all* people who are in authority should be resisted. Since then, Bruce has continually resisted *all* authority figures whether it was in his best interest or not. Because of this decision he did poorly in school and after graduation he has been unable to hold or keep any job for more than two weeks.

In this situation, Bruce's anger at his father was inappropriately transferred through his defense system. He developed protective mechanisms in the form of complexes which led him to experience hostility toward all authority figures. By projecting the problem outside of himself and continuing to place the blame on the authority figure, Bruce, in the end, mainly hurts himself. When Bruce's middle self senses that he is dealing with an authority figure, his dialogue voice, a recording maintained by the lower self but run by the middle self, tells him that this person is exactly like his father. He, too, must therefore be against him so, to protect himself, Bruce must act aggressively. This happens every time Bruce feels that someone is acting like an authority figure whether or not he really is. While the lower self maintains this complex to protect him, we wonder if it really does? It certainly doesn't seem to. While it was initially meant to protect him against his father, his lower self is now applying it indiscriminately to anyone who has any of the same characteristics, consciously or unconsciously, that Bruce's father had. Often Bruce (his conscious self) cannot understand why he (his unconscious self) acts the way that he does. He doesn't understand that his lower self, being a robot, is following orders given to it years and years ago. We often forget that we gave important commands to our lower self, commands which were once essential to remember for our later protection and survival. We may even forget the original experience that threatened us. However, since our lower self never forgets, we will continue to act in response to these prior commands until they are removed. The lower self will do what it is told indefinitely, if the orders are not countermanded.

THE THREE AKA BODIES

The three energies of the body have physical counterparts often referred to in Western terminology as auras, astral bodies or even etheric bodies. In Huna these "energy bodies" are called the *aka bodies*. Much like electricity flowing through a wire has a magnetic field around it, each of the three levels of energy has its own aka body. While each is separate, they are all interconnected. When *mana* is sent to the Higher Self, it must travel by way of the *aka cord*, the cord of aka material that connects the aka body of the lower self and the aka body of the middle self. It also connects the energy of the lower self to the aka body and energy of the Higher Self.

In mythology the *aka cord* is also known as the *silver cord*. This cord attaches our aka body to our physical body. The concept of astral travel relies on the ability of the aka bodies of the middle self or lower selves to leave the physical body and travel anywhere they desire in the Universe. As long as the silver cord remains intact the aka bodies of the lower andmiddle selves can return to the physical body at any time. If, however, it is cut or breaks for any reason, the aka bodies cannot return. It is this silver cord that is severed during the process of dying, making it impossible for the middle, lower and Higher self aka bodies to return to the physical body. This causes the irrevocable loss of the life force, death. This function is also involved in a process which has confounded modern medicine for many years, *NDE, Near Death Experiences.* Many physicians refuse to believe that a person can die and then return to life having experiences of the "other-side." For the student of Huna this is quite simple. As the life force began ebbing and leaving the body, the aka bodies of the lower and/ or middle self separated out and left the physical body, however, the silver cord remained intact. For whatever reason, and there can be many reasons, death or complete loss of vital force did not sever the silver cord. As the physician revives the individual the life force rises and the aka bodies reenter the physical body. The Huna masters have recognized that the aka bodies are essentially exact duplicates of the physical body. The aka body of the lower self has memories but no ability to make decisions, nor the logic to make them with. The aka body of the middle self has no memories but can make decisions and, when away from the physical body and in a solid form, would easily be mistaken for the individual himself. When both aka bodies, middle and lower self, aretogether we have essentially an exact duplicate of the individual himself. This duplicate etheric self has all of the memories of the physical self, and it has the capacity to go anywhere in the universe it wants to simply by thinking it is there. Finally, it retains exact memories of whatever it did or where ever it went.

USING POSITIVE ENERGY FOR HEALING

An important aspect of the role of the physician is to be positive, to create hope and potential of healing. This should not be done falsely, for this would be dishonest. Lying would create negative energy which would either delay healing or stop it completely. Many physicians do not feel that it is honest to be either hopeful or believing in the potential of healing in the face of what appears to them to be a hopeless situation. While being positive entails a sense of clearly understanding what illness and disease are, it also requires that no power be giving to the illness or its process. On a simplistic basis, that means not believing in illness. Often when situations appear hopeless, this negative sense is communicated to the ill person and he or she gives up. Believing in something means that you give it power. People derive power from their beliefs,positive or negative. If they have no belief in an idea or thought, then it has no power over them. The physician who believes in illness and/or disease gives it power over his life and the life of his patient. Because ultimately the outcome of the disease is not really in his hands, and any beliefs he holds is in fact false. His eyes and ears may lie to him. They may only tell him what he wants to believe.

Since the physician doesn't know that his belief in illness is faulty, and instead believes wholeheartedly in his beliefs, he may endeavor to use everything in his power to maintain these beliefs. Often he may find that information and evidence arise which appear to be in direct conflict with his entrenched world view. He may then dismiss or discharge this evidence as erroneous or meaningless. When he sees patients who he never expected to get well, and spontaneously they do get well, he calls it a fluke and discounts it as some sort of error in diagnosis or laboratory testing. In other words, he may discount the situation. Physicians, who are less entrenched in their own personal view of the world, may look at the same situation and think of it as a "miracle," believing that something extraordinary has happened, yet not fully accepting it because it doesn't quite fit the mold and cannot be fully accounted for. Since most illness and disease are simply an intelligent message from the body (lower self) communicating conflict, then indeed, these illnesses are illusions. This is why the enlightened physician can never believe in illness nor give up on a patient until death has occurred. If he docs, hc is not only believing in an illusion but he is giving up without looking for and working on the true underlying cause. If the physician does recognize illness as an illusion, he is then aware, that below the illusion he sees, there is a truth that must be found. If he believes it to be an illusion but still ignores the underlying cause, he loses his ability to see past the illusion. The physician, who recognizes the illusion of illness and disease can move past the obvious manifestations (the signs and symptoms) and look for the specific underlying cause which the signs and symptoms are trying to communicate. He can see the distortion, lies, faulty belief systems, complexes and conflicts which impair the ability of the body to function normally and healthfully. He can only see the process of the illness when he is not blinded by the illusions that bacteria or viruses *caused* the problem. Only then can he appreciate that in the fully healthy individual the immune system is capable of protecting the body in almost all conditions.

The physician who believes in the illusion cannot empower his patient and ultimately turns him into a victim. Because he believes in illness, his patient soon will, along with the patient's family, the community, and the society around him. When his patient experiences symptoms, it is his body communicating with him, and he errononeously believes that he is ill. Because he believes he is ill, and the illness comes from outside of him, he does not listen to what his body is telling him. He cannot see his conflicts. Becuase he cannot see the cause of the signs and symptoms he thinks of as illness, not only does he fall victim to the illusion of illness, he also falls under the power of his ignorance.

If the middle self believes in the illusion enough it can entirely miss the message from the lower self; eventually even the lower self will believe in the illness. If the middle self tells the lower self that it is real, then both will eventually tell this to the Higher Self and the Higher Self will manifest what it is asked for. Without finding the cause and solving the necessary problems, the process progresses. Eventually it robs him of his health and vitality and if not limited or stopped, it can ultimately kill him and destroy his family.

HOW DOES AN ILLUSION LEAD TO ILLNESS

The lower self, convinced by the middle self that illness exists, sets into process the *acting out* of the illness/disease. Initially, the stress mechanism is triggered (we discussed why earlier), finding no real illness (invaders from outside of the self), it begins a process of either turningagainst itself (allergies, autoimmune diseases, etc.) or eventually breaking down in a kind of metabolic exhaustion. The immune system is impaired, the defense systems are instructed that they must let the process happen (for the lower self believes what is happening is *real*), and in time the stage is set for the individual to become truly ill. Once allowed to enter the body, illness takes on a life of its own. When we maintain a belief that illness is real, even if only by believing it we create a *negative force*, a kind of powerful, unwelcome demon. We provide a reason for the lower self to accept its realness and the authority to allow it to exist rather than reject it. If death is accepted as the natural outcome of the particular illness or disease, then it is likely that the illness will progress through all of its symptoms and stages until it reaches a chronic state. Ultimately, the illness will cause the individual to die. One part of the individual may ask for help, possibly for the relief of pain, while another accepts the process as a real process which must cause pain. If the individual believes cure is possible, or even likely, he may, just as if he prayed for it, set in motion the resolution of the problem.

In such a situation, the individual goes to his doctor and is examined and treated. However, hemay unconsciously recognize the doctor's belief in the illness. The combination of his belief and the doctor's belief in the illness, as well as his belief in the doctor, may create a situation where progression of the illness or disease is accepted. If, on the other hand, the doctor does not believe in the illness or believes strongly in the possibility of cure, through treatment, and the patient accepts the doctor's power to heal him, he may well rapidly get better. Because of his desire to get well and his belief in the power (the doctor often has great powers and rituals to support healing) he will take the medications prescribed and, in fact, will soon feel better. In many cases, the patient may have to take medications for the rest of his life in order to halt the progression of the illness. The combined beliefs of doctor and patient that the illness can be controlled, along with taking medication that acts as a kind of ritual and affirmation, will also protect the patient from the natural progression of the illness. The same thing can happen when the doctor fully believes in illness but the patient doesn't. Here a strong belief on the part of the patient plus his recognition of the doctors belief in illness may well act to limit the ultimate affect of the illness and direct its course in a positive direction. After all, the patient is the real healer and it is his beliefs which ultimately control the outcome of the process.

Here again, the taking of medications (see the section on the Ritual of Medication in a latersection) may be used by the patient as not only a form of affirmation, but as a symbol of the power of the medical profession to assist in his healing. Clearly his positive intentions and positive actions in taking the medications are extremely important. It has been my personal experience after practicing medicine for more than 25 years that most people who are seen in medical practice are *cured* within a relatively short time of their decision to come in. Often they are cured even before coming in. One could conclude that once the patient has made the decision to see the doctor and to get treatment his lower self frequently cures him. By his choices and later actions, he has given a clear and decisive command to the lower self to heal the illness and resolve the problem. If the patient has decided that he will go to the doctor only to let him do the work and make the decision, or simply out of fear, it is less likely that he will get the same results.

To the physician who believes in illness, what has been said above is more than likely nothing but *crazy talk*. Since he believes in illness, how could he think otherwise? He would most likely consider anyone who doesn't believe in illness to be a fool, or even a charlatan. Before the Wright Brothers flew at Kitty Hawk, most credible scientists considered flying impossible, only for birds and never for men some said. However, once the

Wright Brothers showed that it could be done, there was a sudden shift in thinking that changed the way we all think about the world. Medical schools have taught for more than three hundred years that illness is real. A whole set of laws and rules has been formulated around this concept. Throughout the ages physicians have felt threatened by opinions that disagree with their own. To some degree, the organization of the scientific community is designed to prevent new information from radically changing the way physicians think. Most new ideas take years to be accepted. Often those in power require rigorous proof of thoughts which differs from their own before they could be accepted. What exists and is believed cannot be constantly changing or the world of the scientist will be in constant turmoil. Yet, in an interesting contradiction every researcher works incessantly for that one breakthrough that will change the way his scientific field thinks and believes.

In the present time and age, medical science still considers illness and disease to be real, and more , effort and proof will be necessary to change their views. However, several new movements including quantum physics, the transpersonal psychology movement and the construct of the new paradigm posed by people such as Fritjov Capra, David Bohm, Stanislav Grof, Albert Einstein, Friedreich Heisenberg, Rupert Sheldrake, are already breaking down the old barriers and changing the world around us. Many well known scientists in many disciplines are demonstrating that mind and matter are not separate but rather part of thesame continuum. Disciplines like psychoneuroimmuno-biology are now breaking down the old medical barriers and changing the topography of what we think of illness and disease.

The devotee of Huna sees illness and disease as an illusion. He sees a positive Universe, with its negative aspects simply as complementary and not as being different (like the heads on a coin cannot exist without the tails). We are now recognizing that illness isn't bad or separate from wellness but instead is a statement of a particular set of needs by the lower self. Negative thoughts, conflicts and negative actions undermine wellness and lead to illness. It can then be said that Illness is a movement away from personal truth. We believe that man was meant to be healthy and filled with the blessings of life and this can only be accomplished when he solves problems and lives in truth. Huna is basically positive because it believes that there is always something you can do, no matter how far the process has gone. Positive thinking, believing in wellness and well-being can always help. Our ability to change our beliefs and take a positive action is the basis of Huna prayer. When our beliefs are totally and truly positive, the illness-disease process can be reversed. If prayer is negative or includes a tone of underlying belief in illness, then it acts as a negative prayer. Not only is help withdrawn, but negative prayers can even accelerate and worsen the unhealthy process.

CHAPTER TWO

Creating Wellness Through Huna

HEALING THROUGH HUNA PRAYER

By uncovering the hidden reasons for the illness, defining the problem and ultimately solving it, the illness process can be reversed and cure can be attained. This only makes sense when one thinks of illness as an Intelligent act of the body trying to communicate conflict that is not being resolved. In this case, illness is an act of the ultimate wisdom of the body/mind in working to resolve conflict. This process is part of our self-healing, self-cleansing capacity. In this context, illness is caused by our faulty belief systems, lies, fears, guilt and sins that have not been resolved or fully experienced. Since the mind/body wants these distortions to be finally set right and resolved, it begins a process of communicating this information to the middle self. It does this in the form of symptoms and signs, *Body Symptom Language*©. The urge to urinate is one such communication. Once we urinate, the symptom, the desire tourinate, disappears. The same is true when our body requires nutrients. It causes subjective symptoms such as hunger and signs such as abdominal growling and gastric spasms (hunger pains) all of which are Intelligent communications from the body telling the conscious self that we are hungry, we need nutrients. Once we eat, these signs and symptoms go away. We see the same type of relationship with many other biologic and non-biologic processes such as defecation, oxygen hunger, temperature sensitivity, sleepiness, a need to move, emotional needs for love, and so on. The concept of an Intelligent body and an Intelligent mind is not new to the medical profession nor to most readers. What is new is our ability to apply this information to the concept of illness and disease.

In Huna, healing is accomplished not simply by changing our belief about something, although this is always the first step. We must also, however, form a specific healing prayer, generated by the middle self as an act of will power through our decision to get well, and our ability to communicate this prayer to the lower self. Usually the lower self will see this prayer as a new command and change bodily processes such as the immune system's ability to respond or function. The prayer may also act on the lower self so that it combines the prayer statement (a seed) with mana (a vital force) and sends these two together up to the Higher Self. The Huna prayer, when it is in the form of a clear visualization of what is desired, willultimately be manifested by the Higher Self. It establishes a pathway for creating a positive image for the future. If it corrects a problem the mind/body wants corrected, it will create a process which will lead to the cure and resolution of all symptoms and signs associated with the originating conflict. The specific details of how Huna prayer works will be presented in the next chapter.

DO EVERYTHING YOU CAN

Is the medical profession doing everything it can for you when you are sick? Is there more that your doctor and the medical community can do that will (1) keep you from getting sick, (2) help you control and eliminate any illnesses or diseases that you may suffer, and (3) keep you well for the rest of your life? What I think you will find is that the medical profession and your doctor are not doing *all* that is possible but, rather, all that they *are willing to do*. In this sense they are not acting on your side. I realize that it may sound heretical to say such negative things about medical doctors. After all, I am one myself. One might ask why I am biting the hand that feeds me. I believe that the question is reasonable so I will give you a reasonable answer. As a member of the medical profession I am responsible to my patients, not to the medical establishment. It is my responsibility to the public at large to report whenthe public interest is in jeopardy.

The problem is not new and it is true that large bodies move slowly in the process of change. I do not believe that what has been done by the medical establishment has been done maliciously. However, if they turn their back on any idea, any technology that can ultimately help more than it can hurt, they are not doing their job. In this sense, they are facilitating illness and therefore are dedicated to keeping you sick.

Once they can and will do *EVERYTHING* that can be done then they are on your side.

THE VALUE OF HUNA PRAYER IN HEALING

As we have stated earlier, Huna differs in a number of ways from Western medicine. Western medicine's primary tools are medications and surgery. These, along with diagnostic testing, are the primary mode of approaching the treatment of illness. While some Huna practitioners may have used herbs, massage and some forms of surgery, the practice of Huna does not generally rely on either medications or surgery as its primary mechanism of healing. In Huna the primary approach to healing comes through identifying complexes, blocks, guilt and sin and eliminating them. This is done in a number of ways. The end goal is to free thevarious energies of the body, to create harmony and balance. Once the blocks to the flow of these energies are removed the body will automatically heal itself. One of the primary techniques used in ancient Huna to free blocked energies is prayer and ritual. The process of freeing energies is generally referred to as *cleansing*. Transforming the negative energies of the past into future, positive energies is referred to as *prayer*. Prayer is used to relieve unseen blocks and to transmute or heal the present and future. Through prayer we can make it known to our aumakua exactly what we want and plant the seeds for it to grow.

In recent years a number of religions and healing systems have reintroduced prayer back into the science of healing. Organizations such as Science of Mind, Christian Science and Theosophy are founded on the use of prayer and the power of thought and faith to bring about healing. In these groups, the concept of prayer differs from that of other organized religious groups. In the Judeo-Christian based religions, prayer is a petition to God to heal the sick. In most of the newer groups, although prayer is still made to God, it also incorporates the concept of seeing the person to be healed as already well rather than asking the Godhead to do the work. Huna prayer, on the other hand, acts still differently. Rather than praying to God to help with healing, one creates a *thought-form* or thought picture of the desired result and then sends this prayer with energy (mana) to the Higher Self to make it happen. In Huna, a prayer is symbolically represented by the planting of a seed. When you plant an apple seed you expect an apple tree to grow from it. The seed contains within it the nature of what is to grow from it. Similarly, when a thought-form is carefully constructed, it will generate what is expected from it. Huna considers thoughts to be packets of energy. Each thought has a form and exists as matter. In other words, in Huna, thoughts are real objects. They have form, shape and substance. The same is true of our ideas and beliefs, for they too are real and bear the fruit of their own nature. They are thought-forms and, if handled correctly, the results they create are directly related to the original nature of the idea or belief. It is for this reason that it is important to be careful of what we think and what we believe. As an old proverb says, "Be careful of what you ask for, for you are likely to get it." This is also the message behind the biblical incantations, "Ask and it shall be given you; seek, and you shall find; knock, and it shall be opened unto you."[13]

In Huna it is essential that you make a specific and clear picture of whatever you desire and then ask for it with the faith in getting it. If you ask for the wrong thing, then your prayer will bring you something other than what you really wanted. What you ask for is manifested by the Higher Self exactly as your thought-form asked for it. Therefore, if your prayer is confused, filled with dualities or mistakes you will not get what you wanted. This is a common problem among people today. The fact is, we always get what we ask for in life. The problem, however, is that most people have no idea of what they really want and therefore what they are asking for. Often they are unhappy with what they get in life. The reason they are unhappy is because they actually asked for the wrong thing. This understanding is important when constructing a Huna prayer. To get what you want out of life you must first develop a clear and precise picture of what you want. This means that, unlike the usual way people pray, to create a Huna prayer one must do a great deal of preparation.

SEEDS OF THOUGHT

It is no accident that the Huna symbol of the thought-form is the *seed*. If we expect a seed to grow to maturity and give us exactly what we want, we must water and nurture it. To ensure a perfect growth, we must do everything that is necessary to make our thought-form spring forth and bloom into what is expected from it. The same is true of all thoughts, ideas andbeliefs. Each one is a seed. Each one can grow and eventually reach fruition, depending on how well we nurture it and what we do with it. A daily charge of mana to the Higher Self is important for the nurturing of the seeds (thoughts, ideas and beliefs) that we have planted. It is no surprise that mana is symbolized as water. Our faith in the final outcome is, in a sense, the soil, the substance or earth, in which we plant our seeds. Our belief in ourself, our self-love and self-caring are the substance of our faith in the creation and burgeoning of what we ask for out of life. Ultimately the secret of getting what we want out of life lies not only in our thoughts, ideas and beliefs but in the words used to ask for them. For example, an individual might ask for power and sooner or later he gets a promotion at his job which gives him more power. However, the promotion may also leave him working more hours than he wanted and this may end up leaving him with less time to spend with his family. While he gets his power, he may be unhappy with it as it takes away from his relationship with his family. Thinking that he must take this new job and do what needs to be done, he dives into it believing that he must do it the way he is told to do it. Over the years he may lose the love and caring of his children, his wife and his friends but he has his power.

A husband tells his wife that he is happy that they are married, that he cares for her and that he adores her but no matter what he says, he never directly says that he loves her. She hears his words and knows they are true, but she still feels unloved. His inability to tell her that he loves her leaves it unsaid and therefore, for her, it is never truly acknowledged. Huna recognizes that what is left undone or unsaid can sabotage what is desired. This is also true about what we hold against ourselves, our angers and limitations, our guilt and fears. These, too, can keep us from getting what we really want out of life.

While most prayers are actually negative, Huna prayers, if set up correctly are entirely positive prayers. This is assured by the care and effort that goes into its creation. To understand why most prayers are negative, let's look at an example. We often hear people make the following types of statements, "I hate my boss, he is such a jerk", "I don't know whether I can do that", "I don't like the way I look at all!" "I must be losing my memory" or "This is what happens when you get old." These are not only negative statements, they are indeed negative prayers. When a person says, "I hope I don't get sick this winter" the lower self, often missing everything but what is expected of it, hears, "I hope (to) get sick this winter." When an individual says, "I always catch a cold during the winter months" the lower self is likely to hear this statement as a command telling it that the individual wants to catch a cold next winter. Remember, the lower self is essentially a child, primitive in its nature and it is also a robot *wanting* and *desiring* to give you anything and everything you ask for.

CREATING A HUNA PRAYER

We have in previous sections discussed some of the basic concepts of the Huna prayer. In the following sections we will look more deeply into this complex subject. It should be clear by now that anything you ask for, intentionally or unintentionally, can essentially act as a Huna prayer. A Huna prayer then is a petition from the middle or conscious self to first, the lower self and if necessary the Higher Self. In the New Testament Jesus tells us, "Ask and you shall receive, seek and you shall find." This is possibly the clearest understanding of what a Huna prayer is. This coupled with the role of the lower self in giving us what we ask for tells us that our Intelligent Universe is designed so that we *can have anything we want and desire if we only ask for it.* As we have suggested previously this includes the bad with the good.

The state of the world and possibly your own life is the way it is because of what we both as individuals and as a society ask for. It is possible that in the past, not understanding what you were doing, you asked, consciously or unconsciously, for things to occur that were not in your best interest. It is now possible with an understanding of how Huna prayers work that you can transform your life and finally get everything you want.

Because of the nature of the Huna prayer we can cause illness just as easy as we can cause wellness. Earlier we suggested that our thoughts were important for through what we think, (as we sow, so shall we reap) we create our personal universe. It should now be clear as to how we do this. Unfortunately, much too often thoughts of illness occur below the level of our consciousness or even subliminally from the society around us. When we accept them blindly, without argument or dispute, without reversing them, they become part of us. One way that we negatively influence ourselves is what we believe about illness. Our experience has shown us that there are many people who strongly believe in illness. Often these are the people who are most likely to become ill. Fortunately, however, not all of these people believe in serious illness. Some examples of this are people who believe that if someone coughs in your vicinity you will catch what they have. People who believe that hypothesis expect to get sick about the same time every year. Additionally, touching something handled by a sick person means that they are going to get sick. Each year, just before winter begins, the T.V. becomes filled with advertisements for cough medications, cold or flu remedies. We frequently hear the news about one person or another who is ill, or is going for surgery, or just died from one or another illness. We are inundated by illness-producing statements and each one is essentially a prayer, if we believe in it.

Huna prayer is an extremely powerful tool for getting what we want out of life. It differsfrom what we usually think of as prayer only in that it is purposefully and scientifically constructed. Usually religious or even non-religious prayer is rarely thought out unless, they are like the Lord's Prayer (which by the way is a Huna prayer because of the way it is constructed) or certain other prepared prayers. What makes a Huna prayer different is that the person who makes it understands what he is doing and plans and prepares the prayer to assure that he *will* get what he is asking for. The underlying principle of a Huna prayer is that you ask for whatever you desire as long as it causes no hurt or harm to yourself or others. Obviously any thoughts of illness would not be part of a Huna prayer.

In the next several sections we will describe to you not only how to construct a Huna prayer but also how to use it. To fully understand how a Huna prayer works, we must once again remind the reader that he or she must consciously (from the middle self) create the prayer and then the prayer is sent to the lower self. This is necessary because the middle self cannot communicate directly with the Higher Self. Only the lower self can make contact with the Higher Self. If the lower self can fulfil the prayer, it need go no farther for it will be done. If the lower self cannot, then we must help it by certain techniques we will describe to create a supercharge of mana to send the prayer first into the aka body of the lower self, then to the aka cord to the Higher Self. If we have blocks, complexes or faulty beliefs systems (sins) existing in the lower self which make the lower self believe that we are either undeserving or unworthy of getting what we ask for, these beliefs can block our prayer and keep us from getting what we desire. To remove these blocks, we must first either release these blocks and complexes or we must create a ritual or ceremony to help cleanse ourself of our sins. When we do this and we are once again worthy of getting what we ask for, then the Higher Self will receive the supercharged mana, and if it accepts the prayer, it will transform the mana of the lower self into Mana-Loa and what we desire will be manifested for us by the Higher Self. If the Higher Self, the aumakua cannot give us what we ask for, then it will turn to the Poe Aumakua to get the desired results. If what we ask for is possible it will be manifested. Huna prayers can be constructed with or without a ceremonial ritual.

With this very basic outline of how a Huna prayer works we will begin our discussion of creating a Huna prayer. We will present Huna prayer constructions with and without ceremonies or rituals.

HUNA PRAYER WITHOUT A CEREMONY OR RITUAL

In constructing a Huna prayer you must first decide what you want, then consider how to ask for it without inserting negatives or distractions. Once this is done, then you must write out your prayer. When the prayer is completed, find a calm and quiet place to present your prayer. While it can be done anywhere and at any time, it is best that the place and time be most conducive for the middle and lower selves to concentrate on the prayer. The following description of the construction of a Huna prayer is taken from Max Freedom Long's description reproduced in Letters on Huna, Mana #4, pages 6-14. A Huna prayer is best performed at a time when your physical, mental and emotional aspects are relaxed so that these parts of you cannot interfere with the creation of the prayer. It is especially important that all business of the lower self, including the digestive process, are clear. Therefore, fasting before prayer is helpful. A Huna prayer session is best set up when the lower self is not working on problems of the day. You will want the full and undivided attention of the lower self to get the best possible results. This is one of the main reasons for using a ritual, as it fully involves the lower self and takes it away from the workings of the problems of daily living.

After the place and the situation are set up, one starts the process by relaxing (meditation is often helpful to expedite this). Now you make a clear and perfect mental picture, a thought-form, which you will use to rebuild your future. When this is completed, keep the picture in mind and begin breathing in through your nose and out through your mouth without holding your breath. Men should pull air into and fill up the top portion of the lungsfirst while women are better off breathing into and filling the bottom portions of their lungs first. As soon as your chest is full release all breath through your mouth. You now offer your picture up to the Higher self. To do this, you give a direct command to the lower self to send your picture to your Higher Self. This breathing procedure is repeated again and again to raise your energy level and create a supercharging of vital force, mana. This is repeated five times. Each time the supercharge of energy is accumulated you call up the memory of your prepared visual picture (thought-form prayer) of the desired condition and cause the lower self to contact the Higher Self. This brings into our consciousness the thought-forms of the desired condition. As before, you visualize your desired condition (picture) which is to be built into the future but see it as a reality in the present. Once again the supercharge of mana carries your mental picture up to your Higher Self. Usually three to five times is sufficient for each sitting. You continue the prayer exercise on a daily basis until you feel that the Higher Self has either received your prayer or accepted your prayer. If the entire picture can be given up at one time, this is fine. If not, it may need to be broken up into several separate prayer actions and performed over several days.

An example of a Huna Prayer might be somewhat like the following. Here an individual has been having some problems with his vision. He realizes that there are things that he has not wanted to see in his life, things that bother and upset him. Yet he knows that he has little choices except to see (these things) or not see (the things he is fearful of). At the same time, he starts working on shedding light on his fears and allowing the light to fall on what he did not want to see in the past. He presents the following prayer:[14]

> "I ask for the strength to open my eyes and my heart to see what
> I previously feared to see. As I see my conflicts, I will set them
> straight. I will take full responsibility for the problems I caused.
> I return my life to full and complete wellness and health.
> These blurred and confused conditions have been the cause of
> my vision problems. I now give praise to my eyes, my mind and
> my body for giving me evidence of these conflicts. From this
> moment on, I see perfectly. As I saw my conflicts, I presently
> see in absolute clarity all that is around me, today, tomorrow
> and everyday in the future. I see perfectly and normally in every
> way, and I shall continue to see perfectly well all of my life."

Huna tradition suggests that a Huna prayer be repeated at least three (but as many times as feelscorrect) with a calm force of assurance and confidence. This is important because each time it is repeated it reinforces the fact that you are not just making a random statement but rather you are demanding (in the sweetest possible way, asking for what is yours) something significant and important. It is most important that your prayer is said with confidence, for if you don't believe it when you say it, then your lower self won't believe it and won't send it up to your Higher Self. The biggest problem people have in relation to prayer is in understanding that getting their prayers answered requires faith and belief, and that what is asked for will definitely come to them. Too often people believe in what they are asking for only at the moment, but after they have gone back to business as usual, they forget what they asked for. While they may expect immediate results, however, this doesn't happen because they no longer believe in what they asked for but only in their desire for results. When they do not get the results they asked for, they may lose faith, denigrate the situation or even stop expecting it. This, unfortunately, is too frequently the case. Your prayer must not only be believed by you, but it must be allowed to occur *when it is ready to manifest* itself. This means having total faith, suspending judgement and actively and expectantly waiting for the results you have requested.

CREATING A RITUAL AS PART OF YOUR HUNA PRAYER

Generally, we don't realize how much ritual we use in our everyday life. Humans are creatures of ritual. We use rituals in courting and mating, in doing housework, at our job, getting to and from work, in play, in school and, as we noted above, even in our medical care. Any situation in which we perform in a set pattern or repetitive actions, as well as anything we repetitively perform, even if it is totally unconscious, is probably a ritual. Activities such as driving, cooking, exercising, dating, making love and eating, are often done almost automatically, without having to think each step through, are rituals. Most all of our habits are also generally rituals. Usually we are not aware of the power these rituals have until they are interrupted or thwarted. The use of rituals increase the power and effect of the Huna prayer. A Huna prayer should never simply be a mental (middle self) process. As such, it has less power and influence over the lower self. To increase the power of your prayers and their effects on your lower self, it is valuable to either use a recognized ritual or to make up a ritual of your own.

Throughout the ages, in both primitive and civilized peoples, music and dance have provided the most recognized and powerful forms of ritual. Physical movement and gesturing are an important part of any ritual. Music, especially a drum beat, provides a rhythmic force which both soothes and trains the body and mind to relax and submit to suggestion. The old saying, "Music has charms to soothe a savage breast," certainly demonstrates its relevance when used in ritual form. While any music can be used, it should not be jarring to the spirit but it should be repetitive and produce a calming effect to be most helpful. Breathing is one of the most important elements of any ritual for it not only brings vital force into the prayer but also meters and creates a rhythm to your movements. The addition of gestures to breathing motions can become the basis of a simple and powerful ritual. The sense of smell can be very important in creating a ritual. Burning or smudging an incense such as sage or any other herb that you particularly enjoy can be valuable as part of your ritual. Water may become an important ingredient in a ritual. Water used to sprinkle or wash is frequently found in primitive rituals. Most ancient Huna rituals included bathing or washing parts of the body such as hands or feet. Water was used by Jesus to wash the feet of his disciples for this very reason. Washing body parts in a ritual generally symbolizes the act of purification of the individual with holy water or mana (energy) before the prayer. Washing away sins makes one ready to receive what is asked for. Taking a warm bath or shower prior to beginning your prayer can be used as a ritual act of cleansing and preparation for the prayer. Washing one's hands or feet can serve the same purpose. Spilling water or sprinkling water may have the power to stimulate the rapid and sure buildup of a mana supercharge.

As we mentioned earlier, fasting prior to prayer is also beneficial. Fasting is a form of sacrifice and is accepted by the lower self as evidence that you mean business. Fasting tells the lower self that you have put off the pleasures of eating to ask for things that are now made more important by the act of fasting. Fasting is also a sign that you are willing to make amends for the hurts and wrongs that you have done to others in the past. A good ritual combines breathing, movement, expressing thought-forms and performing the other activities mentioned above and blending them with a supercharge of energy to convince and support the lower self in transmitting your prayer to the Higher Self. This combination will certainly get the attention of the Higher Self. The process of creating a ritual is easy because *any actions of physical movement or gestures* that you believe will help you get what you ask for is of value. Any ritual can be modified periodically as long as it is not too often and the changes made are logical and reasonable and are done to make the prayer more valuable.

The prayer rite should not be mechanical in nature. For best results, each step should have a specific meaning that awakens and stimulates you and impresses the middle and lower self that you mean business and are worth getting what you are asking for. When the prayer rite is mechanical or boring it is not unusual for people to fall asleep before the prayer is completed. If this happens, change the ritual and make it more active or insert into it a step to refresh yourcharge of mana.

SECRETS IMPORTANT TO THE
PERFORMANCE OF A HUNA PRAYER

To ensure that your prayer works properly and quickly several steps are required.

1. The use of Huna prayer must be accepted, believed and truly desired. Testing the system may not work because the individual always knows that he is testing himself.

2. The prayer-action must be practiced until the lower self has learned the work that it must do. One can't expect that it will know exactly what to do if the middle self has not been interested in it.

3. Repetition is extremely valuable. The prayer works best if repeated at least three times daily. While the exact words do not have to be used again and again, the essence of the prayer should not change significantly or the results may change or be diminished.

4. Before starting your prayer amends must be made for *all* hurts done to others. This is in itself one of the most crucial steps to accepting the healing. As amends are made feelings of negativity, anger and hostility often drop away (assuming the restitution is complete and true). If compensation cannot be made directly, then good deeds, gifts, charity orfasting will help convince the lower self (and the middle self as well) that the debt has been paid and that they are now worthy of getting help from the Higher Self.

5. What is asked for must be good for all concerned and *must hurt no one*. This is very important, for the lower self must be sure that the desired condition is truly good for the individual and that the work to bring it about is worthwhile. The lower self must also believe that the individual is willing to assume full responsibility for all resulting consequences, good or bad.

6. It is always helpful to pray for others or for healing of others as part of your own prayer. However, when a number of totally unrelated things are asked for in the same prayer this is likely to diminish the value of the prayer. When the prayer is confused or cluttered it is less likely to be granted.

7. The more love, self-respect and self-esteem the individual feels and experiences for himself and others around him, the more likely the prayer will be fulfilled.

COMPLETION OF THE HUNA PRAYER

A Huna prayer-action is ended when it feels as though the message has been given to the Higher Self and that the Higher Self has accepted it. It may be difficult to recognize when the Higher Selfhas received or accepted your prayer. In that case, your prayer may be ended when you have repeated it three times. As you become more experienced you may find that you can recognize the acceptance of your prayer by a profound sense of joy or a sensation of a great thrill with a strong emotional component. You may find that your eyes will tear, there may be a feeling of lightness or floating, a sense of love, especially a kind of love for all people, a kind of unselfish love.

When ending each prayer session try to stay quiet and in a state of relaxation for at least an hour afterwards. Allow complete physical, mental and emotional relaxation. This is important to allow the lower self to carry out your instructions. If you return to normal activities too soon the lower self will be recalled to its normal activities and may well leave the prayer-action incomplete.

Max Freedom Long concludes his description of the Huna prayer by stating, "Someday when the practice period is over and one can be sure each time that the prayer-action is completely and properly made, a single request for a desired condition may be enough, and can be allowed to stand while we wait in full faith and confidence for the appearance of the desired condition." He further suggests that the beginner start with simple requests and keep repeating his prayer-action, each time trying to make it more perfect, until results are obtained in the form of answers to his prayers. He admonishes that it does take time, faith and a dedication to getting the results that are desired.

CHAPTER THREE

The Use of Rituals, Sacrifices and Objects in Healing

Earlier we stated that both the lower self and the Higher Self are more likely to accomplish what is asked of them if they have proof of your sincerity. This is not only true in Huna, but it is true in modern medicine, modern religion and life in general. According to Huna, when a prayer is made it is advisable to perform a ritual, offer a sacrifice or involve an object in some way. The underlying intention is to demonstrate your commitment and prove to both the Higher and lower selves that you truly mean business.

RITUALS

A ritual is a series of very specific actions and activities, a ceremony which is used to solemnize some core event. It is often used as an ordeal of preparation, a sacrifice or an action to obtain a specific result. In the sense that we are using it, it is to train the mind and focus it on obtaining aspecific goal. Generally, on a day-to-day basis, our minds are operating on many levels. We deal with making a living, family, our hurts and desires and our needs for the future. The use of a ceremony or ritual focuses the mind so that there is one and only one thing it is paying attention to, the object of the ritual. Rituals transform the individual from an ordinary state of consciousness to a heightened state of consciousness. When this happens we join the universal consciousness and the Intelligence of the Universe. At these times, experience has shown that healing is more rapid and our prayers are more likely to be heard (by us and our Higher Self) and to be accepted. Rituals were known to be a greatly significant part of Shaman healing rites. Often music, especially drums, or dancing were part of these ritual processes. It is likely that this music and dancing actually changed the participants brain function. Some believe that these rhythmic sounds and dancing create a kind of hypnotic trance; others suggest that they only relieve tension, relax the participant and make him more willing to accept suggestion. Still others feel that the music and dancing opens a channel directly into the healing areas of the being and in doing so facilitate healing.

Whatever the reason, ritual was often used as part of healing ceremonies. This was also true in ancient Hawaii. Dance and music, through the vehicle of the Hula, are still used in healing rituals and ceremonies. Another aspect of ritual is chanting. Often used in combination with dance-like activities and music along with repetitive verbal sounds, the chanting of specific prayers had great power. Whether the prayer itself had power or the associated ritual had the power is really unimportant for our needs. What is important is that chanting rituals are a powerful tool in healing ceremonies.

SACRIFICES

It has often been said in our society that, "the value of something is what we are willing to pay for it." We have almost all heard the statement, "You don't get something for nothing." These concepts are well known to most people today. The concept of sacrifice is an extremely old one. It goes back so far into the history of man that no one really knows how or where it started. In fact, it may be one of the Universal *archetypes* which affect mankind. Those that theorize about the significance of sacrifice suggest that there are three possible reasons for its use and its power. One reason, as we stated above, may be to demonstrate the value of the thing desired, for example, what healing has to the individual asking for it. The second, reason is the belief in the necessity of giving up something of value in order to cleanseone's self of sin. This philosophy is at the base root of Huna. The sacrifice frees the individual of his debt created by the sin(s) he has committed. The third significance, goes way back into antiquity and is associated with the recognition of the Universal deity. It recognizes that *all* is consumed by this deity. For example, when we eat, our food is burned by the deity within us, the sun burns gases to give light, etc. In this sense, nothing but God is permanent and we have no true possessions. Therefore, the ability to give up what we "own" is a sign of allegiance, support, respect and submission to the ultimate Deity. His acceptance of our sacrifice allows us to own what we get. "The Gods are pleased."

For our purposes, sacrifice relates directly to the value of what we desire and the cleansing of past sins. When we suggest a sacrifice it is for these two purposes, to show how meaningful healing is to you and to accept the cleansing of the sins and fears that would block you from getting what you desire. We will discuss the process of cleansing in much greater detail in a later section.

THE ROLE OF OBJECTS

Objects have two roles. One is their inherent value in the sense of a sacrifice as stated above. Their other role relates to their physical and material concreteness which becomes symbolic of the tangibility of the ritual process and the acceptance of healing. Just as the lower self gives power to the written word, it also gives power to material things. This is one of the reasons for materialism in our society today. The "solid" object can be used as part of the sacrifice or as part of the ritual process itself to "concretize" the process. The role of the physical object is frequently related to the drama of ceremony. For example, the armaments of war in a military parade, the scepter of sovereignty, the badge of the sheriff and the stethoscope of the physician. These objects have no power of their own; they take power from the meaning that we assign to them. So it is with most objects involved in rituals.

There are, however, some objects which are infused with power. During medieval times amulets, crystals and gem stones, along with other assorted objects were believed to have intrinsic power for healing within them. On the other hand, power most commonly used was put into objects from the outside. For example, the Holy Grail, the chalice used at the Last Supper, was said to have powers given to it by Jesus. Whether the object is inherently powerful, infused with power by its owner or simply believed to have power, the ability to heal is often assigned to inanimate objects. To demonstrate this power, we only have to look at the way in which most official organizations including nations, governments, churches and even the medical profession use rituals, sacrifices and objects to create power and to convince their petitioners or patients of their power. For example, the blessing of the Holy Sacrament, the Pledge of Allegiance, the ritual of the physical examination, the use of the ring in modern wedding ceremonies, the cross of Christianity, payingthe doctor's bills, dues, membership cards or jackets, school emblems, stethoscopes, oto-ophthalmoscopes, surgery, medications, etc. All of these are either rituals, sacrifices or objects which add reality to the individual's belief system. They help him to feel that what he is doing is correct, that he belongs and that he has given something of value to be worthy of the healing he desires and petitions for.

THE RITUALS OF THE PHYSICIAN

In the previous section we suggested that the medical profession as a whole and physicians in general use rituals as part of modern medical practice. We also alluded to the ritual of the physical examination. Before we go further we should briefly discuss these rituals.

Few people, and surely not very many physicians, think of modern medicine as shamanistic. Yet, it most certainly is. While the average medical doctor likes to think he is a scientist, he still continues to refer to the Art of Medical Practice and misses the overall meaning of this concept. While science provides a background and substance for medicine, rituals, objects and sacrifices still play very important roles in the process of healing. Inherent in any ritual are the actions that people must take. These actions, when associated with a specific end result, create a sense of power. The process of healing through medical practice requires a number of such ritualized steps. The patient must decide he has a problem, call thephysician and make an appointment. On the day of the appointment, he washes and dresses (often differently than for his day-to-day activities). He must change his daily routine, traveling from his home or work to the doctor's office and possibly getting insurance forms before he leaves. Once he has arrived at the doctor's office, he announces himself to the receptionist, takes a seat and picks up a magazine to read without being told to do so. He then sits patiently and waits until he is called. Usually if he talks at all, he does so softly or in a whisper. Once he is called, he follows the nurse (often blindly) and then submits himself to whatever he is told to do. He may be asked to take off his clothes (something he would not normally do outside of his home), sit in a small room semi-naked and wait patiently. He is then weighed, his blood pressure is taken, blood may be taken and then he matter-of-factly answers extremely personal questions asked him by the nurse, who is often a total stranger. In a sense, this is a ritual. Generally, it occurs in a slightly altered state of consciousness, as the mood and level of consciousness of the person seeing a doctor is not generally his normal state. He is frequently more somber than usual. He is often slightly, moderately, or even severely afraid. He does what he is told and he is patient about it.

THE EXAMINATION RITUAL

The physician then enters and begins his examination ritual. First, he may greet the patient; however, not all doctors do this. If they are friends the greeting may be warm. If they hardly knoweach other the greeting is often curt and to the point. "Good morning, I am Doctor ——, Please take off your shirt and sit on the table." His mood is frequently matter-of-fact. You know he means business, he has little time and don't cross him. Next, he takes a brief history, "Why are you here today?" He then asks a number of questions important only to him. He may look in your eyes, check your ears, check your reflexes and almost always listen to your heart. The exam may be brief or comprehensive but he is in control and he uses his objects as tools of power. How important these "tools" are in the ritual? It is not unusual for patients to feel that they haven't gotten their "money's worth" if the doctor does not listen to their heart, even if listening to their heart has nothing to do with their specific complaint. Frequently, the patient asks: "Hey Doc, aren't you going to listen to my heart?" An important part of the medical ritual is the prescription of medicine. This is often of great importance to the patient. It is a sign of having a real problem. Our experience has demonstrated to us that if no prescription is given, many patients feel that the physician has done nothing for them, even when there is absolutely no reason to prescribe medication. Another part of this ritual is *The Taking of the Tests*. Few patients are really satisfied if no testsare taken. Ordering a test is powerful enough to cause the patient to forget that he didn't get a prescription. He may consider that he will get a prescription later, after all tests are completed. Here are some of the important elements involved in the modern medical examination. They are remarkably meaningful to the ultimate well-being of the patient. Did the physician touch the patient? Did he give an indication that everything was all right or did he in any way suggest that there might be further problems? How much did he charge for his examination?

Less meaningful today, now that insurance companies often pay for examinations, is the ritual of paying for your medical services. This act often finalized the healing. When the patient himself paid from his hard earned monies, the amount charged for the exam was important. The amount often determined not only how good the exam had been but how likely the patient was to get better. The more the patient was charged (within reason) the more powerful the experience and hence the healing. This is also exemplified by the importance of where the doctor's office was located. Doctors at the Mayo clinic, on Park Avenue or Harley Street were certainly considered better than a neighborhood doctor, even if this wasn't true. People often rejected the word of their local doctor to travel to some mecca of medicine to get healing. Studies demonstrate that doctors who touch their patients during the process of their examination are more likely to get better results than doctors who do not. Physicians often find that patients who are given free service or don't pay often do not get better. Doctors who use no rituals often do not get as good a result as doctors who do. The use of rituals for healing have always been important. Denial of their value, or unwillingness to use them often decreases the value and results of the doctor's services.

There is also a ritual associated with prescriptions for medications. The patient must go to the pharmacy, hand over the prescription, wait for it to be filled, pay for it, take it home and then take the medications according to the instructions. The medications become a *scared object*. They hold the potential of cure, they are powerful, they are prescribed by the doctor, they are part of a ritual and they require sacrifice (spending the time to get them, paying hard-earned money for them and taking them).

Surgery is another type of ritual. It requires the "medicine man" who is all powerful to decide that there is a "disease" and that nothing else will work but surgery. The patient is prepared for surgery, the procedure is explained to him as well as the expected outcome and the risks. He is sent to the hospital, put in a room, stripped of his clothes. Other parties to the ritual (shaman in the form of nurses and technicians) do things to him to prepare him. He may be shaved, food is withheld (everyone knows fasting is powerful medicine), he has special tests done and finally sacred soldiers (the aides and orderlies) come to take him to a sacred place (a surgical suite which he would normally never be able to see). Here, strange things are done to him and eventually he is made to enter a state of altered consciousness. When he awakes he feels sick and he has pain near the area of the diseased organ. He is soon taken to another strange, sacred room where he otherwise would not be allowed to enter and kept there *until* the shaman warriors (doctors and nurses) say he can leave. When he is returned to his room once again he must fast, but the benevolent Gods (doctors) have arranged for the infusion of foods (IV's) and powerful medications for his pain and suffering. When he is once again alert, the physician tells him of the results of the surgery, the Gods were either with him or against him, and his ordeal is over.

Surgery is often seen by the medical profession as a sacrosanct and final act to create healing and reestablish wellness. In Huna, if an individual has created an illness because of guilt or fear from having committed a sin, the more he believes in his guilt the less likely he is to respond to healing measures. At some point, the only way he can forgive himself is to give up a piece of himself — an ultimate sacrifice. Though we understand the concept of *Body Symptom Language,*° we can immediately recognize that conflict, guilt and the pain resulting from them, must eventually require healing, or death may ultimately follow. The body (especially the lower self) creates illness as an Intelligent action to attempt to communicate to the middle self the need for a solution of anunderlying conflict. In doing so it picks an area or organ that gives information about the conflict. Often this is the organ the physician sees as being his patient's problem, as this organ is the focus of the "disease" process. Often when nothing else works, surgery acts as the final sacrifice and the removal of the organ allows atonement, release, relief and relaxation.

Rituals are comforting. They allow the individual to feel safe and to have a sense of direction. Because of this, they reduce stress, they focus the mind and allow concentration on the intended result. Rituals themselves may be therapeutic in that their structure and acceptance by society allows self-forgiveness to occur just through the process of performing the ritual. Lastly, rituals, especially long, drawn-out ordeals, are healing for the discomfort. Conformance serves as penance for the sins which we have committed or simply believe we have committed.

MEDICINE AND THE ROLE OF HUNA (AND RITUALS)

In recent years more and more people have moved away from traditional medical care. The public is not getting what they want, healing, from physicians. Possibly this is because physicians are generally unwilling to recognize that the individual often needs what the shaman can give him. Those in the medical profession separate themselves from their patients, rejecting healing and indulging in and hiding behind science. In the end they ignore the true needs of their constituents. Today as never before in the history of mankind, people are interested in preventive care. Theyalso want to be made part of the healing process. They want safe medicine in the sense that less is more. Not getting these from the medical profession they are turning to nontraditional healers, chiropractors, nutritionists, acupuncturists, holistic doctors, homeopath, spiritualists or other healers. The ritual of the chiropractor, the acupuncturist, the acupressurist, the massage therapist, and the body workers include touching and caring. They are more satisfying and they are not as potentially dangerous. These practitioner do not treat their patients in the cold, matter of fact, or curt manner that physicians often use. They spend, or appear to spend, more time with the patient and generally get to know him as a person. Considering themselves less of a God than the medical doctor generally does, they are more human and often more believable.

Physicians are often so bewildered about illness that they tend to memorize causes and treatments. They look for the worst and force their patient to fear the worst. They so believe in illness that they often are unable to recognize a well patient who has problems or unresolved conflicts caused by the stresses of life. Rather than consider stress or spiritual imbalances as reasons for illness, they turn against the patient and tell him that the problem is entirely in his head or that nothing is wrong with him or worse that he is mentally ill. Being intimidated by stress and spiritual matters, physicians become helpless and instead of providing the specific help their patients need, they instead prescribe unnecessary medications which delay resolution, prolongs symptoms andultimately encourages illness. Since medical science includes no information about the three selves and how they work, it is not unusual for medical doctors to feel confused and helpless even in the face of simple problems. Often they must create "complicated scientific explanations" as to why their patient does not respond to their medical treatment. "The circulation to the area was altered because of a biochemical imbalance and that is the cause of the problem." They become stumped when laboratory and other diagnostic testing (such as x-rays, MRI or CTScan's) comes back normal. They believe that they must have abnormal tests before they can feel comfortable about what they are doing.

We recall one doctor who had for several months felt bewildered about what was happening to one of his patients. When he finally got back an abnormal test which allowed a medical diagnosis to be made, he sighed and then smilingly, turned to his patient and said, "OK! Now that I know that you really have a problem, we can get to work and cut it out." Similarly, physicians may become baffled when one of their patients, for no apparent reason, suddenly gets well from a illness that he was not supposed to recover from. "The stress of the illness must have cured him," one doctor told a patient when his patient's mysterious "life-threatening medical problem" suddenly spontaneously resolved itself. Although the Huna masters had specific rituals for almost all occasions, most of these rituals were lost during the years in which Huna was banned in Hawaii. Of the rituals that do remain and are still practiced by the descendants of Huna practitioners, few if any are available for publication or outside use. The rituals that are used are more for demonstrations of ancient ceremonies than tools for healing. While Kahunas still exist in Hawaii, they are generally not used by the majority of the modernized population. Instead, they are used primarily by the older Hawaiians who remember days gone by, or on occasion, they are used when western medicine fails and the family turns to a local Kahuna to solve a problem that the medical profession could not solve.

As we now move into the twenty-first century and establish a new paradigm for wellness and healing, we will find that Huna provides a system that is both ancient and more modern than the present day "modern medical system." Huna allows us a glimpse at what medicine could look like in the future. The role of the "holistic" movement has been to integrate mind, body and spirit into health care. Huna has provided this for more than two thousand years.

SACRED ENERGY

In previous sections we have discussed the three forms of life energies which are acknowledged in Huna: Mana (vital energy), the energy of the lower self, mana-mana (will power), the energy of the middle self and Mana-Loa, the High Mana or spiritual energy of the Higher Self. The creation of a Huna prayer is intimately connected to these three energies. Without them, Huna prayers cannot be either fully created nor fully answered. Use of our inherent energies and a system for creating prayers are not usually taught in most religious systems that encourage prayer. Because of this, people do not often get what they want. Therefore, many people ultimately lose faith not only in their religious belief system but in the process of prayer as well. The Huna practitioner knows that the middle self cannot directly communicate with the Higher Self. In order to have a prayer answered, the middle self has to first ask and then order the lower self to send the prayer up to the Higher Self. Once the lower self sends the prayer up, the Higher Self can then and only then act on the prayer as the middle self desired and the lower self asked for. The currency of these exchanges are the three energies, mana, mana-mana and Mana-Loa and their sacrifice to the Higher Self and the desire to have what is asked for. This process has been symbolically represented historically by the "burnt offering." In the Bible there are many stories of people sacrificing something they treasured and burning it in a sacrificial fire, or energy. This concept combines a sacrifice, the taking of the life of the so-called sacrificial lamb, the lamb being an object of value which the lower self can understand as being a meaningful gesture and then burning it, that is sending it up to God as proof of our desire to get what we ask for is exactly what Huna prayer is about. The nice thing about Huna prayer is that you don't have to sacrifice anything. Nothing has to die except the lies, guilt and sins we have created during our life. Initially, the middle self must send mana-mana (will power) to the lower self to energize it. The prayer is then infused with mana (life force) to combine with the will to increase its energy and only then is it sent up to the Higher Self. The Higher Self, receiving the combined energies of the middle and lower self is now sufficiently energized (assuming that no blocks, conflict or guilt has taken mana away from the process) to create ample Mana-Loa to generate the energy needed to consummate the request.

If you think about it, all of these steps are quite obvious. If we desire to create something using prayer, we first think about it, then create a plan through our conscious self. When we have accomplished this, our body goes and gets the materials needed and creates the conditions that are essential to producing what we want. Our Higher Intelligence, our inner knowing, then magically brings together our ideas with the materials and substances of the Universe to give us what we desire. The part of us that knows how to make it happen, is the Higher Self. Once we create something, either in our imagination or in our reality, we create it for the whole world, for once our thoughts and actions are manifest they become part of the Intelligence of the Universe. It is exactly because of this belief that the Huna practitioners look at the action of prayer as a sacred offering of energy. The Higher Self, the aumakua, represents the totally loving, utterly trustworthy father-mother parental spirit and all that it gives us becomes part of the totality of mankind. Being totally loving and utterly trustworthy, how could it make something for one and keep it from all others? This would be inconsistent and probably impossible. In this sense, prayer is sacred, for when that which is asked for benefits one, it ultimately benefits all. Our aumakua is also our guardian, for if something is asked for that is destructive, if there is unresolved guilt or if there is a sin that has not been cleansed, it is likely that the prayer will not be answered. To be effective, the aumakua requires that all sin, complexes, and fears be resolved. In this structure all negative things occur through the strength of the will power when energized or dedicated to faulty beliefs.

The Judeo-Christian concept of the Devil does not exist in Huna. Huna does, however, recognize the existence of spirits and they can have evil intentions. These spirits are generally the disembodied aka bodies of the middle or lower selves. The disembodied spirit of the lower self is essentially a diembodied animal nature. The Hawaiians and Polynesians also recognized spirits of which could only be described as archetypical characters of Man. These they saw as Gods. They believed these Gods created them, watched over them. These were their aumakuas. For the most part however the Kahunas believed that evil existed within the person in the form of faulty beliefs and evil thoughts, lies, complexes, fears and guilt. Evil is what we do when we act out of anger, rage, guilt, fear or unhappiness. It is also how we see things when we are unwilling to accept our fears because of weakness. In a sense, evil is no tjust the opposite of good, but it is specific actions that are taken by people or read into events when fear and the unknown goes unchallenged.

Often, if we look carefully, many of the things that we first see as evil turn out to be blessings in disguise. Also, many of the things we first call evil turn out to be lessons of what not to do or how we can do better. Finally, evil can come from the misguided use of the powers we have inherent within us for example, when will is used in a negative way to hurt or take from others. However, almost always, underlying these evils are faulty beliefs, lies, guilt, anger, lack of healthy values and self-esteem.

THE MAGIC FOUNTAIN

The symbolic representation of High Mana (Mana-Loa) is a fountain with water rising from its base shooting into the air and falling back to the ground as a "blessed rain." This symbolism is very old and exists in many cultures. The Huna practitioner, when he is summoning up the great charge of mana that is necessary to send a prayer to the Higher Self, visualizes a fountain with a stream of water rising up from it. When the water reaches a point above his head, this is the key that the charge has been created. As the Higher Self accepts mana from the lower self, a transformation occurs, *waiola* (the living water or holy water) is created. This "holy water" (energy) can be used to better the individual's own self interest. When excess is available, it can be used to help others or to better mankind. This second part is often returned to us in the form of the "rain or blessing." In the Bible it is stated that God "rains manna from heaven." This biblicalterm suggests that this manna symbolizes food and water; the Huna mana symbolizes pure energy that is created by the food and substance of the Universe.

Huna teaches the use of these symbols to create the supercharge. As we stated earlier, the creation of this charge is related to the use of the breath and breathing. Breathing in brings an unlimited quantity of energy from the Intelligent Universe we live in. Breathing out releases excretory products and expended energy. The visualization of the fountain allows the building up and concentration of sufficient mana to permit the prayer to be sent up to the Higher Self. Finally, the "rain of blessing" symbolizes the granting of the wish and the benefits it brings not only to the person who made the wish but to all that rely on him and to mankind in general. These principles have been embodied in many ceremonies. It is often the secret behind the prayers offered before sacramental wines are poured. It is given as an offering for the return of the blessings "rained" upon them. It is also the secret behind the ceremony of saying grace before a meal. It is, in fact, the secret behind all of the sacrifices and offerings associated with prayers, no matter how far they have become separated from the wise ones that initiated them. The taking in of energy from the Universe, its use for our needs and the rain of blessing created by its use, create a cycle which returns it to the universe to be used again when needed. This cycle is referred to as the *Cycle of Life*. Inherent in this cycle is the role of healing to *bring back to wholeagain*.

This aspect of Huna is in strong contrast to the sterile approach of modern medicine which holds that the power of healing lies only in the hands of the physician. Healing must be performed by use of medications, some of which are actually poisonous to our system, and surgery. The sterility of modern medicine creates no place for the identification of the cause of a specific problem nor the need of the individual to solve his problems and grow from them. Prayer is only sanctioned when all else has failed. The cause of illnesses in modern medicine is generally seen as being outside of the individual where he has no power over it.

In a sense, modern medicine, because of its many rules and rigid beliefs, its dogma, acts more like a religion than a science. Often, physicians act more like members of a cult, with rigid views and closed minds, than as practitioners of an art which requires mastery, skill, growth and learning. The physician who employs Huna involves the patient in his own care and healing. The patient, not the practitioner, heals the illness. The formerly ill person is empowered and grows from the experience. The physician who practices Huna principles teaches his patient to pay attention to what hethinks, what he believes, how he uses his words and who and what he gives power to. The physician who teaches true prevention, that once learned, allows for permanent health and well-being is truly a physician to the people. The physician who empowers his patient practices the true art of healing.

WHY RITUALS FAIL

It is not unusual for rituals to fail to work. If you are to construct a ritual or use a ritual, it is important for you to understand why they fail. The two most common reasons for failure is the feeling that you are not worth getting what you desire and a lack of belief in the ritual or prayer itself. When either of these situations exist, you may be willing to try using a ritual and even initiating and performing it but then find the process breaking down. Eventually, you will find that you have been unable to get the results you desired. Generally, in a case like this the petitioner soon considers the ritual tedious, time consuming or inconvenient. Rituals can be sabotaged by external forces. Family, friends, physician or the church may undermine it. In the past we have seen physicians subvert their patient's needs to use prayer, religion or alternative health care modalities because of the physician's own prejudices, fears or anxiety over losing desired revenues. (As this would hurt the patient, it would be a sin on the part of the physician.) Patients themselves frequently sabotage their own rituals for many reasons. Consider the patient who stops taking medicine before the prescribed course is over or the individual who refuses to follow his or her physician's instructions. Once again, prior sins, guilt and fears are often involved. The individual who *needs* his illness or maintains an "illness mentality" may obstruct his own recovery because of fears of losing his illness and hence his secondary gains (although he rarely recognizes that this is what is happening). Often his secondary gains cover up feelings of inadequacy or of unworthiness.

We have repeatedly stressed that you will only get the results you desire if you believe that you are worthy of getting results. In this case the ritual itself is not the problem. It is the individual's diminished sense of self-esteem and worthiness that are the culprits. Ritual and prayer may not work if they are not addressing the right problem or the wrong result is desired. It is also possible that the problem has advanced beyond the individual's ability or capacity to use prayer or ritual. It is also important to watch for thoughts about matters of daily living creeping into your prayer or ritual. When this happens the prayer and ritual become incomplete and their value is diminished. Periodic refreshing of Mana helps your middle self to be able to control the lower self and prevent the drifting of your thoughts. Often the use of will power is necessary to minimize your rambling thoughts. This requires energy and will take your mind off of your prayer or ritual. It's better to make your prayer and ritual interesting, positive and enjoyable so that your mind won't drift. Once will power is required to focus the lower self into action, the prayer becomes downgraded to a mere affirmation. And, as you know, affirmations must be repeated hundreds, even thousands, of times in order to get results. Huna prayer, when done efficiently and right, need only be offered once for excellent results.

CHAPTER FOUR

Creating a Healthy Future

The impact of Western science on our modern society is great. Over the past 50 years with the combined efforts of medical science, we have made enormous gains in reducing deaths due to secondary infection, childbirth, catastrophic surgical problems, injuries, cancer, heart disease, genetic illnesses, exposure to the elements and many other areas through highly sophisticated medical treatments. Working together with Governmental agencies and consumer advocate groups, we have succeeded improving the ability to improve the quality of food, water, consumer goods and even the air we breathe. There is certainly no question that we have extended the longevity of the average man and woman.

Yet many people still believe that we have done little for the quality of life or the ability to prevent illnesses related to stress. As the morbidity and mortality rates due to physiologic and traumatic injuries fall, the chances of death or disability because of Stress Related Disorders rises. Stress andits many consequences are rapidly becoming major problems to the medical profession. While the many illnesses caused by stress could be greatly impacted by the medical profession, they are not. While the many illnesses caused by spiritual and transpersonal conflicts could be impacted by the medical profession, they are not. One major reason the medical profession is less effective then they are is that they greatly limit themselves by their Newtonian-Cartesian view of the world. Another reason is their unwillingness to use every bit of knowledge, every discipline, every bit of wisdom from every group of peoples who have ever solved problems. Instead, they would rather see themselves as an elite club, the science club, needing proof of things that can never give us proof. While waiting for proof that will not come, and scowling at those that want to look to the past, people get sick, then sicker and even die.

Most physicians are unaware of the individual and combined roles of the human mind, body and spirit. Because they are unaware of these parts of man, they are unable to use them and the knowledge of other healers to heal their patients. Instead, they prefer to wall themselves off treating and refusing to grow. Huna, presents an opportunity for the Western doctor to look at a system that integrates the whole being in such a way that it allows the physician to become a healer.

What is most valuable about Huna is that it can be used to prevent illness. Hence, the Western oriented medical doctor can, with little study or effort, transform him or herself into a wellrounded and enlightened physician, a healer, one who heals rather than treats. The physician, who practices Interventive Medicine, doesn't have to give up his skills, he doesn't have to use roots and herbs, he doesn't have do anything but increase his understanding of human beings and his abilities to prevent illness before it starts and reverse it more rapidly once it has already taken hold. The medical solution, treatment, may still be the answer for some people, for some stage and level of problems, but there will be less illness and more healthy people if he masters what the ancients knew. In all cases we still *strongly suggest* that health problems should be evaluated and handled by *competent physicians*. We still believe that everyone, young and old should have periodic complete examinations. We still believe that *all necessary* laboratory and diagnostic testing should be performed and *a clear diagnosis should be established* before any form of treatment, Huna or medical should be started. We still believe that *knowing exactly what the problem is, is always most important, and that finding the underlying conflicts that cause the illnesses is essential for diagnosing the problem and creating a final cure.* There is no question in our minds that *knowledge is the key to success.*

However, we believe that through the use of Huna and Huna prayer physician and patient working together will better be able to fully and completely eliminate illness and disease. Through using the understandings of Huna, the average individual will also better be able to control his life and positively affect his well-being and health. For the physician or patient who is interested in learning more about Huna we have included a bibliography which includes an excellent listing of a number of beginning level books about Huna. Studying these books will give you a even greater understanding of the value of Huna.

While most often we think that the future will have all the answers we need, Huna shows us that the past has a great deal to offer to us. By better understanding the teachings of the past we may well be able to change our future for the better. For the lay reader our comments about the problems of the medical profession is not to diminish what they do but rather to support you in taking a more active role in your own medical and health care. For the physicians who have read this work take heart, and continue to grow, go beyond the medical establishment, use Huna and whatever other disciplines you find open to you to support your patients, your family and yourself in a bright journey toward health, wellness and well-being.

Bibliography

BOOKS ABOUT HUNA

Max Freedom Long Series (A few of the more important selections.)
Recovering the Ancient Magic, MFL, Huna Press, $6.95
**The Secret Science at Work*, MFL, DeVorss Publications, $11.95
**The Secret Science Behind Miracles*, MFL, DeVorss Publications, $11.95
The Huna Code in Religion, MFL, DeVorss Publications, $12.95
Growing Into the Light, MFL, DeVorss Publications, $7.95

Serge King Series
**Kahuna Healing*, Serge King, Ph.D., Quest Books, $8.95
**Imagineering for Health*, Serge King, Ph.D., Quest Books, $8.50
**Mastering Your Hidden Self*, Serge King, Ph.D., Quest Books, $7.95
Urban Shaman, Serge King, Ph.D., Fireside Books, $9.95

Miscellanous Authors
**Huna, A Beginners Guide*, Enid Hoffman, Whitford Press, $12.95
The Heart of Huna, Laura K. Yardley, Advanced Neuro Dynamics, $9.95
Gestalt and the Wisdom of the Kahunas, Bethal Phaigh, DeVorss Books, $5.95
   Mana Magic, John Bainbridge, Barnhart Press, $5.95
   Kahuna Magic, Brad Steiger, Para Research, $10.95
**Seekers of the Healing Energy*, Mary Coddington, Healing Arts, $9.95

Books Not Directly About Huna But Encompass Major Aspects of It
·*The Adventures of Self Discovery*, Stanislav Grof, M.D., SUNY, $16.95
·*The Holotropic Mind*, Stanislav Grof, M.D., Harper Collins , $20.00

These books are not the only books about Huna but rather a selection that covers the very basic aspects. The * books we found particularly valuable in the Introduction of Huna to the beginner. The other books might well be read after completing the introductory series.

The two books by Stan Grof are particularly interesting and are more for the advanced reader. While specifically not about Huna directly, the material presented is considerably more valuable after a basic understanding of Huna. Grof, an unusually advanced medical practitioner and a psychiatrist, deals in the area of Transpersonal Psychology. His Holotropic therapy delves into the vast world of the subconscious (lower Self) and connects it to the supra-conscious aspect of man (the Higher self). Like Huna itself his work transcends the domain of Western Medicine and enters into the area of Healing.

BOOKS ON HEALING

The following are a list of books which I have found particularly interesting and valuable in understanding Healing as versed to medical treatment. These books represent the new more realistic direction that medicine will take into the 21st Century. I will use the * to represent books that are interesting and ** for those books which have of special value. The • is used to represent books which are of a more advanced level. This list is by no means exhaustive but rather only represents introduction into the area of Healing. The symbol (O) represents older books and suggests that the price listed is an old price and may have changed.

Books of General Interest
*Love, Medicine, and Miracles, Bernie Siegel, M.D., Perennial Library, $8.95
From Here to Greater Happiness, Joel and Champion Teutch, Price, Stern, Sloan, $2.95 (O)
Handbook of higher Consciousness, Ken Keyes, Living Love Center, $2.95 (O)
The Road Less Traveled, M. Scott Peck, M.D., TouchStone (Simon & Schuster), $9.95 (O)
Psycho Cybernetics, Maxwell Maltz, M.D., Wilshire Book Co., $2.00 (O)
*Healers on Healing, Richard Carlson, Ph.D. & Benjamin Shield, Tarcher, $10.95

Non-Scientific Poetry and Prose that Will Enliven Your Spirit
*Notes To Myself, Hugh Prather, Real People Press, $2.95 (O)
*Anatomy of an Illness, Norman Cousins, Bantam Books, $4.95 (O)
*Illusions: Adventures of a Reluctant Messiah, Richard Bach, Dell, $4.95 (O)

Consiousness and the Many Demensions of Life
**Stalking the Wild Pendulum, Itzhak Bentov, Destiny Books, $8.95
**On Mechanics of Creation, A Cosmic Book, Itzhak & Mirtala Bentov, Destiny Books $8.95

Society Medicine and Healing
o**·*The Tao of Physics*, Fritjof Capra, Ph.D., Shambhala, $5.95 (O)
**The Turning Point, Fritjof Capra, Ph.D., Bantam Books, $11.95
**Uncommon Wisdom, Fritjof Capra, Ph.D., Bantam Books, $12.00

Books About the Mind and How it Works
•*Stations of the Mind*, William Glasser, M.D., Harper Row, $12.95 (O)

1 Remember there was a time when "modern medicine" asked its patients to believe in blood letting and leaching. The modern surgeon always asks his patient to take a leap of faith in believing in him and his judgement that an organ or some part of his body must be removed.
2 John 14,11.
3 Serge King, *Mastering Your Hidden Self, A guide to the Hanoi Way*. A Quest

Book. p. 22.
4   Serge King, Mastering Your Hidden Self p. 22.
5   Same.
6   Printed with special permission from Enid Hoffman and Whitford Press. Taken from *Hanoi, A Beginners Guide*. See the bibliography.
7   Enid Hoffman, *Hanoi A Beginners Guide*, see the bibliography.
8   The suffix in parenthesis was added by the authors.
9   Max freedom Long, *The Secret Science At Work: The Hanoi Method As a Way of Life*. See the Bibliography.
10 By *outer meaning* we refer to the middle self, or the meaning we commonly thinking of. Later in this discussion we will refer to the *inner meaning* we refer to the hidden or lower self and Higher Self meanings.
11 Long, *The Secret Science At Work, The Hanoi Method As a Way of Life*. Pages 88-91.
12 In this case a false knowing.
13 Matthew 7, 7., also in Luke 11, 9.
14 The example just stated is simply an example. It is not a real case history.

High Probability Selling